D1243775

Dedicated to my Lord and Savior Jesus Christ, the one true Hero who brings life to all who come to Him in faith. May this book bring you honor and glory, for You alone are worthy.

CONTENTS

HEROES, VILLAINS, AND OTHERS IN BETWEEN
52 Biblical Character Studies

By Cameron Walcott

HEROES, VILLAINS, AND OTHERS IN BETWEEN
52 Biblical Character Studies

****

He was an old man now, sitting in a cold, dark prison, knowing that his time on earth was drawing to a close. He had traveled the world and seen things that few would ever have believed possible, but those exciting days must have seemed far in the past. Almost all his friends had deserted him; he spent most of his days alone, with only a Roman soldier chained beside him as his guard. Still, he wrote to his faithful follower, giving him an encouraging message and asking for his coat to be brought to him before winter. Most important, however, was his last request, "Please, make sure you bring my books. Don't forget the books!" The old man was the Apostle Paul, and he was making this request to Timothy only a few months before he would die. The Apostle never stopped studying, never lost his passion to learn, right up to the time of his death.

****

Why should we study Biblical characters?

When you are in school, you study a wide range of characters from history. Growing up in the United States, I remember studying great heroes such as Christopher Columbus, George Washington, and Abraham Lincoln. We learned much from their lives and saw qualities we could emulate and ways we could seek to be like them. Of course, we didn't only study history's great men; we also studied those who had brought great death and turmoil to the world. Learning about men like Alexander the Great, Adolf Hitler, and Mao Zedong is also important, as their failings can be analyzed and their mistakes avoided. As the saying goes, "Those who do not learn from history are doomed to repeat it."

From the title of this book, you can tell that we will be examining a wide range of Biblical characters. Great men and women such as Abraham, Joseph, and Esther will be considered, as will failures like Saul and Ahab. Moreover, there are several men we will consider who don't fit neatly into either category, men who had many successes in their lives but also made great mistakes. What we must realize is that it is profitable for us to study all of these men and women, the bad as well as the good.

And that's why I love studying Biblical characters, and I hope you do too. The Bible is God's Word, and should be the very foundation of our lives (Matthew 4:4, 7:24). We need to understand that absolutely everything that is in the Bible is there for a reason. It's there to give us hope, instruction, and encouragement; there to show us the way to knowing Christ and being more like Him. The Bible is not only made up of propositions and theories, but primarily of stories. And these stories are real life events that happened to real life people in a real life world. We can see ourselves in these stories and imagine what we would have done in their situations.

We are told that the things that happened in the lives of Biblical characters should all serve as examples to us (1 Corinthians 10:11). Through studying the men and women of old, we can be inspired by their faith and challenged by their sacrifices. We can be warned by their mistakes and admonished by their foolishness, as we see seeds of these same flaws in ourselves.

While it is true that we often learn things "the hard way", this should not be our goal. Rather, we should seek to learn life lessons not by repeating mistakes made by people but by avoiding them; not by ignoring their positive examples but emulating them. I can illustrate this with my two-year-old son, Caleb. As a toddler, he moves quickly around the house and has little sense of danger. He often tries to touch the stove or climb into unsafe positions. As a father, what is my attitude? I don't say, "Caleb should touch the stove, then he'll learn not to do it." I don't think, "Let's have Caleb fall from that high chair, then he'll learn not to climb." Rather, I instruct him, I stop him, I warn him, so that he can learn things in the easiest way possible. It's inevitable that he will make some mistakes, experience some pain, and learn from these experiences, but we never encourage the mistakes. We only learn from mistakes when we have ignored the better way to learn. The best way to learn is always the path of obedience!

Psalm 119:105 famously tells us, *"Your word is a lamp to my feet and a light to my path."* Let's allow the light of God's Word to guide us through our walk with Him. The study of these Biblical characters will be invaluable in pointing us onto God's path. As we saw in our opening, the Apostle Paul never lost his passion for studying the ways of God, and may the same be said of us. There is always more to learn, more to gain, from the lives of the people in God's Word. May this book be an impetus that puts us all on the path of studying these men and women throughout our lives.

What's the best way to use this book?

Hopefully, this book can have several different uses. It contains 36 different Old Testament character studies, and 16 from the New Testament for a combined total of 52 short chapters. Each individual character study highlights one outstanding quality in the person's life. We find in the Scriptures that certain people are often noted for certain qualities, and we try to stick by those qualities in this book. For example, in the life of Job we learn about patience, and in the life of Elisha about the anointing. Whether you want to study a certain character or a certain character trait, both are possible.

This book is intended to be both for young people and old people, new believers and experienced Christians. To this end, there are several different ways in which it can be used, three of which we will suggest here:

1) Devotional Life.
Each character can be studied for personal devotion purposes. Perhaps you would like to read one character each day and pray about and meditate on the lessons learned throughout that day. It also could be possible to read several characters in one day and quickly read the book, then go back and review those who were especially meaningful to you.

2) Personal Study.
The book can also be used as an impetus for personal, in-depth study. Though each character's outline is rather brief in this book, references are provided where you can look into the relevant Scriptures on your own, believing God to give you fresh insights from His Word. The outlines are by no means comprehensive, but can serve as a guide from which you can launch into personal study and gain new understanding about the character's life.

3) Sermon Outlines.
Each character study could also be developed into a sermon. Four easy-to-use points are included

with each study and can be readily expanded upon. These outlines could be especially helpful to a young preacher/teacher (for example, a cell or small group leader or a Sunday school teacher).

However you use the book, it is my prayer that the things written here will come to life in each one of us. May they not just be words on paper, but a reality in each of our lives. We study not just so we can know more, but we study to *become* more, to become more like Jesus. Let it be true in each of our lives.

CHAPTER 1: ADAM AND EVE - BEGINNINGS (GENESIS 1-5)

Have you ever tried to watch a movie when it was already halfway through? Or maybe you started watching a TV serial after a few episodes had already passed. If you liked the show and you're like me, you probably wished that you hadn't missed the beginning. Joining midway through caused you to miss some vital information.

As a Christian, I've got good news for you! You don't have to "miss" the beginning. God has left us detailed information on how everything (the world, our faith, our hope) began. And that is our main theme in this passage - "Beginnings." Adam and Eve were the first people God ever created and in them we see the start of several important qualities of man. Understanding our beginning will give us a much clearer idea of our present and future condition, so it is vital to look into their lives and our world's beginnings.

1. *The beginning of the world* (1:1-1:25). In six days, God created everything - the sun, the moon, the stars; sharks, leopards, and monkeys; oranges, trees, and rice fields. Everything was formed through the creative power of His spoken word. Just look around you and notice all that God has done. Nothing was created by chance or random coincidence, but we know that God is the active agent in all creation. There is nothing He cannot do.

2. *The beginning of man* (1:26-2:25). God created Adam in His own image, out of the dust of the ground. God wanted a being who was like Him, who could understand Him and have fellowship with Him. God then took one of Adam's ribs to create Eve, the ideal complement to Adam. Adam and Eve were perfect in God's sight. Man was created with purpose, to know God and glorify Him, and this purpose applies to each one of us. Your life is valuable because you were created by the King.

3. *The beginning of sin* (3:1-3:13). God placed Adam and Eve in the Garden of Eden, a beautiful garden where all of their needs were met and they were given only one instruction; do not eat of the Tree of the Knowledge of Good and Evil. Satan appeared to Eve in the form of a snake and deceived her to eat of the tree's fruit, and Adam also chose to disobey and partake of the fruit of the tree. Through their pride and curiosity, they disobeyed God by eating the one fruit God had told them to avoid. Their sin opened the door to sin for the entire human race, and since that time everyone has been born as a sinner. Adam and Eve further compounded their mistake by hiding from God and using fig leaves to cover themselves. Since that time, sinful man has continually tried to hide from a holy God.

4. *The beginning of redemption* (3:14-5:32). This is the last and most glorious beginning. God declared to Satan that a descendant of Adam and Eve would crush Satan's head; that descendant of course was Jesus Christ! Furthermore, God replaced the leaves Adam and Eve used to cover themselves with the coats of an animal, showing that death was needed to atone for sin. Abel's acceptable offering of his animal to God in chapter 4 further illustrated that a truly Great Sacrifice was coming to redeem man from his sin; that was the Lamb of God, Jesus Christ.

Pay careful attention to the story of Adam and Eve. It's important to understand our beginnings. The stories you will read are unlike any other story book; these stories are all *absolutely* true and are a foundation of our faith in Christ. We know that we did not come from a "big bang" or a monkey, but we were created by the hand of God, and He had a plan for our salvation from the very beginning of the world. Our faith in our foundation gives us faith for our future.

CHAPTER 2: NOAH - GRACE (GENESIS 6-9)

Have you ever lost something that you just could not find? Maybe it was your cell phone, your homework assignment, or your favorite shirt. I remember one time when I lost my keys and tried to find them by looking in every part of the house. After hours of searching, I finally found them inside the pair of shoes I had worn that day!

Noah was a man who found something more valuable than anything else, and this was the key to his life, **"Noah found grace in the eyes of the Lord (Genesis 6:8)."** Grace is God's undeserved favor (we get something good that we do not deserve) and also his divine enablement (we receive power to do something we cannot do). We learn several qualities of grace from the story of Noah.

1. Grace overcomes evil (6:1-7:9). Noah lived in an extremely wicked time and place. Because of the evil in every person's heart, God decided to send a flood that would destroy the earth. The entire creation would be wiped out and God would have to start over. However, God found Noah, and through God's grace to him the human race was preserved. God instructed Noah to build a giant boat in which Noah would be safe, along with his wife, his three sons, and their wives. Moreover, God decided to preserve the animal kingdom as well, by sending one pair of every unclean animal and seven pairs of every clean animal into the Ark. It was a very, very crowded boat! The grace of God to Noah was more powerful than all the evil in the world.

2. Grace can be rejected (7:10-8:3). Noah spent an amazing one hundred years building the Ark. God sent the flood that destroyed the earth on the very day he, his family, and the animals boarded the Ark. Everyone not in the boat died. Noah had surely warned them that judgment was coming and gave them opportunities to repent, but the people hardened their hearts and continued their wickedness against God. This illustrates to us that God's grace can be wasted if we do not repent. He is a gracious and merciful God, but if we continually reject Him He will bring judgment against us. That's why it is always important to obey God today in everything He speaks to you. Also, it is vital that we warn others - our God is a holy God. The tower of Babel is another example where wicked people rejected the grace of God.

3. Grace gives us God's direction (Genesis 8:1-8:12). Torrential rain fell on the earth for forty days and forty nights before stopping. Noah and his family waited inside the ark for a little more than one year before they found out if the earth was dry enough for them to exit the Ark. Three times Noah sent a dove out of the ark to see if it was safe to leave; on the third time, the dove did not return, showing that the earth was now a clean place as the dove was a clean animal. The dove is a type of the Holy Spirit. If we will learn to rely on God's grace and not our own selves, He will lead us by His Holy Spirit as well.

4. Grace brings us into God's promises (8:13-9:29). God then gave Noah a promise that He would never again destroy the world with a flood. As a sign of that promise, He showed Noah a rainbow. Every time we see a rainbow, we can remember that promise of God and be assured of His grace towards us. Noah and his family then repopulated the earth, and through the line of Noah Christ was born, bringing blessing and promise to all mankind. We receive the blessings of God only through grace!

Let's be amazed by the grace of God, that would bring such blessing to Noah and his family. Ask God to cause you to be someone like Noah who receives His grace.

CHAPTER 3: ABRAHAM (PART 1) - RIGHTEOUSNESS BY FAITH (GENESIS 12-17)

Many nations have one man whom they look to as their "founding father." In Singapore (where I currently live), that man is Lee Kuan Yew; in America (my home country), it is George Washington. Did you know that as Christians, we also have a founding father? The Bible tells us that man is Abraham, the father (under God) of all who would believe (Romans 4:11-16). His life is so important, so rich, and so thoroughly covered in the Scriptures that we will spend the next two chapters examining his faith.

The key verse of Abraham's life is Genesis 15:6, where we read that Abraham, "believed in the Lord, and God accounted it to him for righteousness." We thus learn an incredible lesson from our father Abraham, and that lesson is this - righteousness comes by faith. We do not become acceptable to God through our good works or activities, but through believing in Him. Faith is a substance that is given to us from God; it is the assurance that what God has spoken He will surely do. When we have faith we do not merely hope that God is there, but we know that He is. There are four main qualities of righteous faith that we will see in this chapter.

1. *Faith causes us to go (Genesis 12:1-14:24).* When Abraham was 75 years old, God called him to leave his home city of Ur and go live in the wilderness in a tent. Ur was the world's most advanced city at that time and Abraham was comfortable living there in his old age, but God told Abraham to leave so that God could bring him into a new place. Abraham's faith caused him to obey God and go, even though he did not know his final destination. We see over and over that Abraham's faith went wherever God sent him, whether in choosing land (chapter 13) or going to war (chapter 14). Let's have faith to go and do the things to which God is calling us.

2. *Faith believes God's promise (Genesis 15:1-21).* Many years after Abraham left his home, God appeared to Abraham. God promised Abraham he would have more children than could be counted, even though he was now more than 80 years old and had never had a child. Abraham did not consider the fact that he was over 80 and naturally unable to have children, but simply believed God's promise. Because of that, God counted him as a righteous man. Do you believe God when He gives you "impossible" promises?

3. *Faith overcomes mistakes (Genesis 16:1-16).* This chapter records one of the great sins of Abraham's life. His wife Sarah, noting that she was no longer able to have children, asked Abraham to have children instead with her servant Hagar. Abraham did so, and Ishmael was born. It was his attempt to fulfill God's promise through his own power, and it was disastrous. However, God did not discard Abraham for his sin but restored him because of his faith. This encourages us that righteousness is not something that comes from inside of us, but instead is rooted in the righteousness of Christ as we believe in Him. So do not feel guilty for past mistakes, but trust God to restore you as you have faith in Him.

4. *Faith enters into covenant (Genesis 17:1-27).* Abraham's faith led him into a covenant, or promised

agreement, with God. After his mistake with Hagar, God promised Abraham once again that he would have a child with Sarah. The sign of this covenant was that all the men of Abraham's house would be circumcised. Abraham followed this sign and entered into this covenant with God. God wants to enter into covenant with you as well, where He makes promises and you obey His command.

Let's realize that righteousness comes only by faith. We could never do enough good works to make us righteous in the eyes of God; the best we could do would always pale in comparison to Him. Yet God gives us His very own righteousness when we have faith in Him. Abraham made mistakes but never lost his faith in God; may we likewise be inspired to believe in Him always.

CHAPTER 4: ABRAHAM (PART 2) - SACRIFICE OF FAITH (GENESIS 18-22)

This week we'll continue reading about the life of Abraham, the "founding father" of our faith. In the last chapter you saw how Abraham left his home to go to the wilderness. God had promised Abraham both a land and descendants more numerous than could be counted. Abraham believed God's promise, even though he had no children and he and his wife were past the age where children could be borne. God considered Abraham to be a righteous man not because of his works but because of this faith, and thus entered into a covenant with Abraham. We will see four more aspects of Abraham's righteous faith in this chapter.

1. Faith intercedes (Genesis 18:1-19:38). Abraham and Sarah were visited by two men (actually angels) to confirm that they were going to miraculously give birth to a son. These angels revealed to Abraham that the cities of Sodom and Gomorrah were going to be destroyed by God for their great wickedness. Abraham then gave us a picture of intercessory prayer, pleading with God not to destroy Sodom (where his nephew Lot lived). Due to Abraham's powerful prayer, God agreed that if even ten righteous people were found in the city, he would not destroy it. However, there were not ten righteous in the city, and God destroyed that area. God did honor the prayer of Abraham by saving Lot and Lot's two daughters. Abraham's prayer brought safety to his family and helped bring about the will and purpose of God. As we have faith in God's goodness and power, we will intercede for our families, churches, schools, cities, and areas of influence as well.

2. Faith brings healing (Genesis 20:1-18). Abraham and Sarah then went to dwell in the land of King Abimelech, and Abraham was afraid that Abimelech would desire the beautiful Sarah and thus kill Abraham. Abraham lied and said Sarah was his sister, so Abimelech took Sarah into his harem (though he never touched her). God then judged Abimelech for this by shutting the wombs of all the women in his house. After Abraham had repented for his sin in lying to Abimelech, he prayed and asked God to heal the wombs of the women, and God did so. It is the first time physical healing is mentioned in the Bible, and it shows us that as we pray in faith, the sick can be healed.

3. Faith produces results (Genesis 21:1-34). When Abraham was 100 years old, his son Isaac was miraculously birthed by his wife Sarah (who was 90 years old). It was now about 25 years since God had first spoken to Abraham, yet the promise still came to pass. Abraham and Sarah rejoiced in the birth of their only son, which was completely impossible in the natural. Yet as we have faith in God's promise, the "impossible" becomes history, the "supernatural" becomes natural, and the miracle will always come. Faith is not a "maybe", but a definite, clear "yes." It always produces that for which it was given.

4. Faith gives all back to God (Genesis 22:1-24). Many years after Isaac was born, God told Abraham to sacrifice his son back to him. Even though Abraham did not understand the command, he obeyed God and prepared to offer Isaac as a burnt sacrifice. God rescued Isaac and told Abraham not to follow through with the sacrifice, as Abraham had now proven that he feared God by not withholding his only son. When we have true faith, we will be willing to give to God whatever He asks from us. Isaac was a blessing from God, but Abraham valued obedience to God above His blessings. We should do the same.

From the life of Abraham, it is important to remember that faith is not just an emotion or a feeling; it is a living reality. God wants this reality to bring fruit in our own lives, so let's be inspired by the faith of our father, Abraham!

CHAPTER 5: JACOB - TRANSFORMING POWER OF GOD (GENESIS 25-32)

I remember one of my favorite toys when I was younger. It was a shiny, red and white airplane, with pointed wings and a prominent nose. It was also a robot, with powerful shoulders and a menacing face. What toy could it be that was both an airplane and a robot? The answer, of course, is that the toy was a Transformer.

Transformations are an incredible thing to see, no matter what age we are. One of the most remarkable phenomena in nature is how a lowly caterpillar transforms into a majestic butterfly. But if transformations are marvelous in the natural, they are all the more awesome in the spiritual. We serve a God who transforms lives. Jacob, the grandson of Abraham, is a prime example of this - he was changed from being a lying thief into a prince of God. In this section we will look at four transforming lessons we can learn from his life.

1. God can transform a bad beginner (Genesis 25:1-34, 27:1-46). Jacob had troubles right from the beginning of his life. He was born alongside an older twin brother, Esau, and they had conflict even during their birth. After they had grown up, Jacob selfishly tricked Esau into selling him the birthright of the elder son for a bowl of soup. Later, Jacob (with his mother's help) deceived his father into believing he was Esau, so that Jacob could receive the blessing of the firstborn. Even the name Jacob meant "crooked" or "deceiver." His life was full of lies, trickery, and deceit.

2. God can transform a selfish follower (Genesis 28:1-22). Still, God loved Jacob and had a plan to use him to bring forth the redemptive line of the Messiah. Esau had rejected God and God thus rejected Esau. Therefore, God appeared to Jacob, showing him a ladder reaching up to heaven. God promised His blessings on Jacob, and Jacob replied that he would follow God if God helped him, blessed him, and provided him with food and clothes. In other words, Jacob gave God selfish conditions on which he would serve Him, showing himself to still be a bad role model at this point in his life. We should serve God with love unreservedly, not based on meeting conditions.

3. God can transform through a difficult situation (Genesis 29:1-31:55). Jacob was on the way to his father's homeland to find a wife when he met his Uncle Laban. Jacob agreed to serve Laban for seven years in order to marry his daughter Rachel, whom Jacob loved. However, Laban deceived Jacob and gave him his elder daughter, Leah, to marry instead. Jacob ended up serving the deceptive Laban for twenty years; during his time of service, Laban dishonestly changed Jacob's wages ten times! God used the deceitfulness of wicked Laban to show Jacob how terrible it was to tell lies! And God can use difficult circumstances, even wicked people, in our own lives to teach us spiritual lessons.

4. God can transform into a new character (Genesis 32:1-32). Jacob finally left Laban, bringing a large family with him. God then appeared to Jacob, in the form of a man. This "man" began wrestling with Jacob, and they wrestled all through the night. Jacob realized this was not really a man but was actually God, and would not let go until he was blessed. God was pleased with the persistence and determination of Jacob and declared that he would have a new name, "Israel", meaning "prince of

God." He was no longer a liar, but was now a prince in God's sight, with an upright character! Jacob was forever changed and did not return to his sinful ways.

We can be inspired by the story of Jacob. If you have been difficult in the past, realize that God makes us into new creations (2 Corinthians 5:17). Ask him to transform every part of your sinful nature today.

CHAPTER 6: JOSEPH - GOD'S AWESOME PLAN (GENESIS 37-45)

Have you ever had something happen to you that you thought was a disaster, but it turned out good in the end? Maybe you missed your bus, but then you ended up meeting your friend at the bus stop. Or perhaps your favorite restaurant closed down, but then an even better one replaced it. You may even have been forced to prematurely leave one country become a refugee in another, but then you met your future wife in the interim (okay, maybe that one only happened to me)! In the natural, things that seem disappointing initially very often turn into great blessings, but it's even more true in the spiritual for followers of Christ.

We serve a God who turns every curse into blessing (Nehemiah 13:2). He is a God who is in complete control of every situation and He specializes in turning loss into victory, sickness into health, and sadness into joy. This truth is excellently illustrated in the life of Joseph, our character in this week's reading. Joseph was one of Jacob's 12 sons, the great-grandson of Abraham, and he carried the promises and blessings of God. Joseph was a young person during the story we read about this week, and is an excellent example for us to follow. There are four qualities to his life that we can emulate.

1) Joseph was a dreamer (37:1-11, 40:1-41:36). Joseph received spiritual understanding from God in dreams. He was even able to interpret the meaning of the dreams of others. He was a dreamer not only in the sense of having natural goals but also in the sense of his dynamic relationship with God. Joseph was a prophet who had a listening ear and understanding heart to know what God was saying. Ask God to cause you to be a dreamer; plan great things for God, and listen to God so He can reveal His plans and purposes to you through supernatural means.

2. Joseph was excellent in all he did (39:1-6, 21-23, 41:37-57). Whatever place Joseph found himself, he excelled. Despite all the unjust things that were done to him, he always strove to be the best that he could be. Other people around him (even the unrighteous) saw his excellence and he was promoted in every place that he went. Joseph's strong spiritual life shone through into natural reality. The foundation of his life was his strong faith in God, and that faith had great impact on his surroundings. We should seek to excel in the natural also, not as our main goal but as a way of showing the work God is doing inside of us.

3. Joseph was morally pure (39:7-20). Joseph was a slave in the house of a man named Potiphar. Potiphar's wife became interested in him and tempted him to commit fornication with her. When tempted with sexual sin, Joseph ran away from the temptress. He realized that it was his responsibility before God to be pure. Therefore, he did not play around with sin but ran away from it. We should also run away from youthful lusts (2 Timothy 2:22). Do not stay around moral temptations but instead run towards God. Stay away from those things (certain TV shows, movies, music, magazines, etc.) that lead you toward lust.

4. Joseph was faithful through fire (37:12-36, 42:1-45:28). Joseph had several terrible things happen to him in his life, any one of which would have caused a normal person to give up. First, he was sold into Egypt as a slave *by his own brothers*. Next, he was placed into prison by his master, to whom he had only done good. Finally, he was forgotten by those he had helped to get out of the prison. However, Joseph never gave up but remained remarkably faithful towards God. When he revealed his true identity to his brothers, he realized that what his brothers meant for evil God had meant for good, declaring that God was in control. Joseph had tremendous faith in God's goodness in every situation.

We can be like Joseph, realizing that God is always faithful and has a good plan for us. No matter how faithful Joseph was, God was always more faithful, and God will always be more faithful than we can imagine. He is a God of love, and His plans towards His children are good. They will come to pass, as we are faithful to Him!

CHAPTER 7: MOSES (PART 1) - THE DELIVERER (EXODUS 1-7)

Water is an essential element to life. If you study the great civilizations of the world, you will find that almost all of them were founded based on their proximity to a water source. Water is needed for drinking, bathing, and cooking; moreover, most people just enjoy being near the water! It's fun to dive, to swim, and to splash in water. Of course, when you're swimming in a river, you're never really sure what you're going to find. Sometimes you see fish; sometimes you see seaweed; sometimes you may even see a shoe! But what was the greatest water discovery in history?

I think the answer is simple; it was the baby Moses! He was found floating in a basket in the Nile River by Pharaoh's daughter. In fact, the name "Moses" means, "pulled out of the water". From this humble beginning, Moses became one of the most remarkable men in history. He lived to be 120 years and was the leader, deliverer, and lawgiver to God's chosen people, the Jews. He is the author of the first five books of the Bible (Genesis - Deuteronomy). We will spend the next two chapters on the life of Moses, focusing on his role as a deliverer. God used Moses to lead his people out of bondage and slavery in Egypt. We are also called to bring deliverance and salvation to our generation that is bound by sin. We will start by looking at four points from the life of Moses on being a deliverer.

1. The Deliverer must first be delivered (Exodus 1:1-2:10). After the death of Joseph, the Egyptians began to fear the Israelites and made them their slaves. The Egyptian Pharaoh noticed that the Israelites kept increasing in number and declared that all the newborn males were to be killed. Moses was born at this time. His parents were people of faith, and therefore hid Moses instead of allowing him to be killed. They put him in a basket where he was found by Pharaoh's daughter and amazingly raised as her own son. He was delivered from certain death in a miraculous way. Likewise, if God is going to use us to bring deliverance to our generation, we first have to be delivered from our own sin and death.

2. The Deliverer must endure disappointment (Exodus 2:11-2:25). Moses was brought up as a prince of Egypt. When he was 40 years old he decided to stand up for his people (the Israelites) and killed an Egyptian who was abusing an Israelite slave. He thought that the Israelites would accept him as their leader and savior, but they rejected him. He ended up being forced to flee into the desert, where he spent the next 40 years watching sheep in the wilderness. It was an extremely humiliating and discouraging experience, but Moses endured. We will go through times where it seems like we have failed, but we must keep our hope in God.

3. The Deliverer must accept responsibility (Exodus 3:1-4:31). After this, God appeared to Moses in a burning bush and told him he was to lead the Israelites to freedom. Moses had now been thoroughly humbled and made a series of excuses on why he could not do the job. God reminded Moses that He was the One who had made man and given them ability, and in the end Moses agreed to go. When God calls us, we must believe His promises and do what He calls us to, even if it seems impossible.

4. The Deliverer must have courage (Exodus 5:1-7:25). Moses stood before the mighty Pharaoh and all his court and commanded him to let God's people go, with nothing in his hand but a shepherd's staff! It was amazing courage, as Pharaoh easily could have had Moses killed with just a word from his mouth. Furthermore, even after Pharaoh rejected Moses' plea and turned the Israelites against him by increasing their burdens, Moses stayed firm. He continually told Pharaoh that he must let God's people go. Likewise, we cannot be afraid of the threats of people but must trust only in God.

Part 2 of Moses' life will be featured in the next chapter! God turned Moses, the "excuse-maker" into a "captivity-breaker," and He can do the same with us!

CHAPTER 8: MOSES (PART 2) – THE DELIVERER (EXODUS 8-14)

One of the most effective plays in basketball is the "trap." In this play, the defense allows the offensive player with the ball to dribble towards the sideline. Once he is against the sideline, two defensive players then surround the man with the ball. He is then unable to move toward the one direction because he would be out of bounds, and unable to move in the other direction because of the swarming defense. It can truly be a hopeless situation, as the ball carrier is stuck with nowhere to go! The defense very often is able to steal the ball.

As we continue our study of Moses, we will examine a time in his life when he was placed in a "trap." We will receive instruction from Moses on how we should react when we are in a seemingly hopeless situation. Just as Moses was a deliverer to his generation, God has called us to deliver our generation from the power of sin and Satan. Will we answer the call as Moses did? This chapter is our second and final one in the study of Moses, focusing again on his role as a deliverer, which is but one part of his remarkable life. Continuing from the last chapter, here are points five through eight on the life of God's deliverer.

5. *The Deliverer must have power (Exodus 8:1-10:23).* Moses was a man who had a position of power with God. Because Pharaoh would not let the children of Israel go free, God determined to bring judgment upon them. Plagues such as swarms of frogs, death of their cattle, and darkness fell upon the land of Egypt; there were a total of ten plagues. Moses was the channel through which these supernatural signs took place. God wants us to be instruments of his miraculous power as well; gifts of miracles, healing and faith can be used to turn our world upside down.

6. *The Deliverer must not compromise (Exodus 10:24-10:29).* While these Ten Plagues were falling on Egypt, Pharaoh tried to compromise with Moses on four different occasions. These compromises would have given the Israelites only limited freedom. Moses rejected each one. We need to have that same determination to not settle for any compromise with the world, but to wholeheartedly seek the vision God has placed in our hearts.

7. *The Deliverer must be saved through the blood (Exodus 11:1-13:22).* The last plague upon Egypt was the slaying of their firstborn. The Israelites were protected from this plague, but only if they kept the feast of the Passover and spread the blood of the sacrificial lamb over their doorposts. Moses kept the feast with his family and they were protected from death. After this plague, all of Egypt was in mourning and Pharaoh finally let the Israelites go. The blood of the Passover Lamb represents the blood of Jesus Christ, Who died for our sins. If we are going to deliver our generation, we must go forth knowing that we are protected and victorious through His death. We boast only in the cross.

8. *The Deliverer must trust God for the impossible (Exodus 14:1-14:31).* After letting the Israelites go, Pharaoh once again hardened his heart and decided to go after them. The army of Egypt, with their horses and chariots, thus chased the defenseless Israelites and trapped them against the Red Sea. The children of Israel were all afraid and knew that they could be wiped out by the army.

However, Moses had faith that God would do the impossible and told the Israelites to wait for God's deliverance. God then caused the Red Sea to part in two, and the Israelites were able to walk across on dry ground! After the Israelites had gone across, the Egyptian army was destroyed when the water came back to its original position and drowned them. The same God who held the water back for the Israelites is the same God who brought the water back upon His enemies. God had given His people a tremendous miracle and freedom. Moses believed God for this impossible miracle.

What impossible things does God need to do in order for your generation to be saved? Believe Him for them, and the impossible will be done! Let's be inspired by the amazing life of Moses.

CHAPTER 9: JOSHUA - LEADER BY FAITH (DEUTERONOMY 34-JOSHUA 24)

Have you ever tried to knock a wall down? How about even putting a hole in a wall? I remember once when one of my cousins and I were playing nerf basketball inside one of the rooms of my house. My cousin went up for a slam dunk, only to lose his balance, fall out of the room, and kick his foot straight through the hallway wall. Fortunately, it was only a small hole and we were able to patch it up quickly! Regardless, actually knocking a wall down is very hard work. It can take hours of labor, even with the very best tools.

Joshua was a man who knew a very effective way to knock down walls-through faith in God! The walls of Jericho fell down as Joshua and the people walked in faith. Joshua led the people of Israel to victory after victory and ultimately possession of the Promised Land. He was a leader of faith, and there are four areas of his life we will look at in this chapter.

1. Joshua learned through small responsibilities (Exodus 17, 24, 32). Joshua started his ministry not as the leader of Israel, but as a servant to the previous leader, Moses. He assisted Moses in many ways, even when he had to wait on him for hours and even days at a time. Joshua was called to be a great leader, but first he had to be faithful in small areas. It is the same for us today. Before God uses us for greatness, He is looking for faithfulness in small, everyday matters (Luke 16:10).

2. Joshua listened to God's instructions (Deuteronomy 34-Joshua 5). Joshua received several prophetic words before he became the leader of Israel. God spoke to Joshua through Moses and others, telling him to be strong and courageous. The Lord Himself even appeared to Joshua, in the form of a mighty warrior. He gave Joshua battle plans and Joshua obeyed. It is a good thing to receive prophetic words that will give us guidance and strength for the days ahead, and it is vital that we learn to hear God's voice and obey the instructions He gives us.

3. Joshua led through the impossible (Joshua 6-22). The Israelites were often faced with "impossible" situations in their possession of the Promised Land. Joshua led the Israelites to one miraculous victory after another. The most remarkable was when the Israelites defeated the people of Jericho. Jericho was surrounded by thick walls and was an impenetrable fortress. However, God told Joshua to have the people march around the city seven times, and on the seventh day the walls fell! The Israelites were then able to take possession of the city. Another time when the Israelites were defeating their enemy, Joshua asked God to cause the sun to stand still in the sky so they would have time to complete the battle. God granted Joshua His amazing request and the sun did not set! Believe God for miracles in your life and the lives of those you are leading.

4. Joshua left a legacy for the people (Joshua 23,24). Joshua victoriously led the children of Israel into possession of the Promised Land during his lifetime. During his final days, he called all of Israel together and gave them a last challenge. He declared that his house would serve God, and implored the people to choose to serve God as well. He left a godly, faith-filled example for all to follow. Let's live our lives in such a way that others will be inspired to give their all to Christ. Leave a legacy for all who will come after you.

Joshua was a leader whose life still inspires people today. He led not through natural wisdom but through the faith of God. God has called each of us to be a leader in one sense or another, great or small, so let's look to use our influence to point people to faith in God.

CHAPTER 10: DEBORAH - THE WORD OF GOD (JUDGES 4-5)

"I'll go, but only if you're going!" Have you ever said that to someone? Maybe you were considering whether to go to a certain restaurant or movie. Maybe you had been invited to go on a trip, and you weren't sure if you would have a good time or not. But you knew if your friend was going, it would be worth joining. If you are a follower and not a leader, you probably make statements like that all the time.

Barak is an example of a man in the Bible who made this kind of statement. He was the general of Israel's army but he refused to go to battle and fight for their freedom unless the prophetess and judge of Israel, Deborah, went with him. Deborah was a tremendous woman of faith who was filled with the Word of God. It is amazing that a battle-hardened general would rely on a woman for strength in war, but Deborah carried the anointing of God upon her life. She knew how to bring victory through the prophetic word. We will look at four areas of Deborah's life to see how God can use His word through us as well.

1. *Deborah was not afraid of difficult circumstances (Judges 4:1-9).* Deborah became the judge, or leader, of Israel in a time when they had been oppressed for 20 years by the people of Canaan and their wicked king, Sisera. The Canaanites had 900 iron chariots, while the Israelites had none. In the natural, there was no possible way the Israelites could defeat this overwhelming enemy. However, Deborah knew that God was not limited by the Israelites' limitation; He could do the miraculous. She told her general, Barak, to prepare the Israelites for war. Never be discouraged by the difficulties you face, but realize that God is able to do whatever He has promised you.

2. *Deborah knew the timing of God (Judges 4:10-16).* The evil Canaanite king Sisera heard that the Israelites were building an army and came to destroy them. Deborah heard from God that this was the day for the Israelites to defeat Canaan, and Deborah gave Barak the message. It is important that our ears are open to God and we know when He is leading us to pray, witness, and conquer for Him. When God says to do something today, we must not wait until tomorrow to obey. Learn to be prompt in following God's timing.

3. *Deborah realized God did not have to use the naturally strong (Judges 4:17-24).* Barak told Deborah he would not go to battle without her. Because Barak was not willing to just obey God but first had to lay down this condition, Deborah declared that he would not have the honor of defeating Sisera; rather, a woman would. This came to pass during the battle. The Israelites, through the anointing of the Holy Spirit and the promise of His word, crushed the Canaanites, and evil Sisera ran away from the battle. He was not caught by the mighty Barak but rather by a woman named Jael. She killed Sisera in his sleep and the Israelites were finally free. Do not assume that God has to use the strongest, most intelligent, or best-looking person to defeat the enemy; He can use anyone who yields to Him.

4. *Deborah rejoiced in God's salvation (Judges 5:1-31).* After God saved Israel from the Canaanites, Deborah led the people in a glorious song, celebrating God's deliverance. The Israelites then had

peace under her leadership for forty years. Make sure that you celebrate the great things God has done in your life. Give Him all the glory for the times He has brought His Word to pass.

Let's learn to hear from God and speak forth His Word as Deborah did; we can bring revival to our generation!

CHAPTER 11: GIDEON - TRUST IN GOD (JUDGES 6-8)

If you've ever climbed a mountain, you know that you need to be careful where you place your weight. Sometimes you might be tempted to put your trust in a small branch or loose rock, just because it's the closest thing to you. However, if you do that you're going to be headed for a painful fall! Successful mountain climbers (which I am not!) learn to rely upon powerful ledges, strong tree trunks, and other immoveable objects.

In our Christian life, we need to learn to place our trust in God, and God alone. All other objects of trust are like a weak twig; they cannot truly support us. Jesus is the solid Rock of our salvation and we can trust in Him at all times. Gideon was a judge of Israel who illustrates for us the need to trust in God. He was a great man of faith who led Israel to many amazing victories. Nevertheless, he had some failings in his life when he stopped trusting in God and started trusting in others. Gideon's life illustrates for us that we should trust in God over the following four different things.

1. Trust in God over signs (Judges 6:1-40). The children of Israel were being ruled by an evil nation called Midian. This nation robbed the Israelites and led them to great poverty. While in this situation, an angel of the Lord came to Gideon and told him that God would use him to lead the Israelites to freedom. This promise seemed impossible to Gideon. He asked God to fulfill a series of miraculous signs before he would believe God, and God fulfilled the signs! Gideon then knew God was on his side and gathered an army to fight Midian. Even though God granted Gideon the signs, it would have been better if Gideon had simply believed God's promise without giving Him conditions. It's dangerous to ask God for signs; let's trust God's Word alone.

2. Trust in God over numbers (Judges 7:1-25). Eventually Gideon gathered a huge army of 32,000 men to challenge the Midianites. However, God decided the army was too big, as the people would then trust in their own strength. He ended up leading Gideon to reduce the army to only 300 men. This paltry number left them no natural chance against the huge army of Midian, but God granted the Israelites a tremendous miracle. Without even using any weapons, they defeated the Midianites and drove them from their land. Gideon didn't trust in the strength of his numbers but in God and was rewarded with tremendous victory. Never trust in your own resources or abilities but only in God.

3. Trust in God over friends (Judges 8:1-21). Not all of the men of Israel helped Gideon in his victory. Some stayed behind when they should have gone to battle and accused Gideon of being at fault. Gideon learned that he could not rely on other men to help him. It is good to have friends along the way to help us, but our ultimate confidence must never be in these other people; it should be placed only in God.

4. Trust in God over idols (Judges 8:22-8:35). After God had given Gideon great victory over the enemy, he responded by forming a golden object that the people of Israel began to worship. He accomplished many great things in his life but left behind a mixed legacy because of his establishing of this idol. Let's make sure we never trust in any of the idols of our age - finances, materialism, entertainment and a host of other things to bring us joy and happiness. Let's learn that true life comes when we trust in God alone.

Trusting in God brings us everlasting strength. It is so important that we don't give God conditions or tests, but simply trust all He has promised us in His Word. He is altogether lovely and true, and is worthy of our complete loyalty and trust, both now and forever.

CHAPTER 12: RUTH - FAITHFULNESS THROUGH FIRE (RUTH 1-4)

One of my favorite places to visit in the nation of Singapore is the Singapore Zoo. Inside the zoo is an area simulating the Great Rift Valley in Ethiopia, and inside this display is a large group of baboons. The baboons are amazing to watch as they jump, run, eat, and interact with one another. One amazing thing about watching the baboons is the tenacious way that the baby baboons hold on to their mothers. They cling so tightly and remain with the mother wherever she goes. It's incredible to see!

Ruth was a woman in the Bible who had this same kind of tenacity. She followed her mother-in-law, Naomi, even through difficult times. She never let go of the call of God on her life, and from her example we learn many lessons about faithfulness. In this chapter, we will examine the life of Ruth to see four things that faithfulness causes.

1. Faithfulness causes us to endure disappointment (Ruth 1:1-22). Ruth and Orpah were two ladies from Moab who married the sons of Naomi. After about ten years, Naomi's husband and both of her sons died. Naomi decided to return to her home country of Israel, telling Ruth and Orpah that they should remain in Moab and marry new husbands and have a better future. Orpah decided to turn back to her old life, but Ruth would not. She told Naomi that she would go wherever she went, live wherever she lived, and follow the true God. She was faithful to her mother-in-law Naomi, but more importantly she was faithful to God! She endured a tremendous disappointment in the death of her husband, but did not turn her back on God's ways. We should follow Ruth's example. We may go through difficulties in life, but God will provide us grace to remain faithful to Him.

2. Faithfulness causes us to work hard (Ruth 2:1-23). After returning to Israel with Naomi, Ruth went to work in a field to provide food for Naomi and herself. It was difficult, humiliating, and dangerous work, but Ruth did not turn away. She gathered enough food every day, and worked so hard that the owner of the field, Boaz, even gave her special privileges and portions. Faithfulness is not just an internal thing - it must show through our outward actions as well. Are you showing faithfulness in your natural responsibilities in areas such as school, work, and home duties? Ruth did, and these outward actions revealed her faithful heart.

3. Faithfulness causes us to wait for God's timing (Ruth 3:1-18). Ruth had now caught the attention of Boaz, who also was one of the kinsmen for Naomi's family (meaning he had the right to marry her daughter-in-law). Naomi instructed Ruth to present herself to Boaz, and she did so, presenting herself humbly at Boaz's feet without making any demands upon him. Boaz saw Ruth's humility and instructed her to wait for him to redeem her. Ruth did so patiently. Faithfulness will cause us to wait for God's timing and not try to rush things according to our own desires. So often we are tempted to demand things be done according to our timetable, but a faithful person waits for God's. When we are faithful, we will find it easier to trust in God's faithfulness, and will learn to trust Him in all things.

4. Faithfulness always causes us to come to fruitfulness (Ruth 4:1-22).   Boaz ended up choosing to marry Ruth. They had a son together named Obed, who was the grandfather of King David! Even greater, many generations later Jesus Christ came to earth as a man from this same line of Ruth. Ruth was greatly rewarded for her faithfulness. She could have returned to Moab and her name would be forgotten in history, but instead her story will forever be inscribed in God's Word. Ruth was faithful to Naomi when it seemed there would be no reward, and God caused her to be extremely fruitful. She was faithful not for the reward but simply because it was the right thing to do, but God made sure she got her reward!

Ruth went through tremendous trials and difficulties in her life, but her reward was enormous. She was not even born a Jew, but became the most notable "outsider" in the line of Christ because of her faithfulness. Let us be inspired to be faithful in all things as Ruth was.

CHAPTER 13: SAMSON - POWER OF GOD (JUDGES 13-16)

Electrical power is an essential element of modern life. Most of us like to carry our cell phones, mp3 players, digital cameras, and even laptops with us wherever we go. However, these items need power in order to function! There are few things more frustrating then needing to make a phone call and discovering that your cell phone is out of power (I don't know this from personal experience but several people who are close to me seem to have a powerless phone almost every day!). Different forms of power are needed for everything we do in a day – many of us need it to even get out of bed in the morning!

Power is also necessary in our spiritual lives. True power comes not from ourselves, but from God. Probably the most famous example of a powerful man in the Bible is Samson, the focus of our study in this chapter. God's strength flowed through Samson in incredible ways. He was a mighty warrior and led the Israelites to several victories over the Philistines. However, though Samson was very strong on the outside, we will see that he had serious character flaws that revealed an inner weakness and kept him from fulfilling God's full purpose in his life. We will consider three qualities of God's power this week.

1. God's power comes through consecration (Judges 13:1-25). Samson's father was a man named Manoah. Manoah's wife was barren, bringing great sorrow to them both. However, an angel appeared and promised them a son, declaring that the boy was to be a Nazarite, specially consecrated to God his entire life. He was to be God's servant, and one sign of his consecration was that his hair was never to be cut. Samson grew up living a life specially devoted to God, and God responded by giving him great power. If we want the power of God in our lives, we need to be willing to surrender every area of our lives to Him. God can bring us great deliverance, even out of barren or dry times.

2. God's power overcomes enemy strength (Judges 14:1-15:20). As Samson became a man, he was well-known for remarkable feats of strength. He helped deliver the Israelites from Philistine oppression, one time killing one thousand enemies with a donkey's jawbone. Another time he caught three hundred foxes with his bare hands, and released them to destroy the Philistine crops. No matter how many men the Philistines sent against him, Samson was able to conquer them through the power of God. Through this truth we discover that God's power in us is able to tear down the works of the enemy. No matter how big the obstacle, we can overcome it when we are going forth in the will of God and are clothed in His Spirit and power. We can evangelize, pray, and preach without fear in any situation through the power of God, and see mighty miracles of healing, deliverance and salvation.

3. God's power needs to be internal and not external (Judges 16:1-31). For all of his strength on the outside, Samson became a very weak man on the inside. He was never able to overcome the sinful power of lust. First, he married a Philistine woman, instead of an Israelite as God had commanded. He then fell in love with the Philistine prostitute, Delilah. He ended up telling her the secret to his power (his consecration, shown by his long hair), and she betrayed him by telling the Philistine men.

They cut his hair, thus depriving Samson of his power and he was blinded and taken as a prisoner. Samson's hair grew back while he was in prison, and in his last act he knocked down the pillars of a building where thousands of Philistines were celebrating and mocking him. As the building fell, Samson killed thousands of Philistines, along with himself. Samson never overcame his sinful lust, and in the end was destroyed by it. We don't only want to do great works for God but want to allow Him to change us on the inside and give us true strength - the strength of holiness.

Samson's life is very important for us to study. It should serve as both an encouragement and a warning. All things are possible through God's power, but we can lose it all if we do not care about holiness. Let's have both power and purity!

CHAPTER 14: JOB - PATIENCE (JOB 1-42)

Have you ever had a bad day? Perhaps you got stuck in traffic or missed your bus. Maybe your computer broke down or you lost your cell phone. It could have even been something serious, like the loss of someone close to you or a disaster that struck close to home. The fact is, all of us will experience bad days in life. But how will we respond to them?

Job is a man in the Bible who had a tremendous response to an incredibly bad day. He was a righteous man, whom God had blessed with riches and a large family. However, in just one day, disaster struck; all that he owned was destroyed, and his sons and daughters died. Job did not despair, however; he remained faithful to God through his trial. He is an example of patience that we can all follow (James 5:11); he did not rise up in anger against God but stayed faithful through the worst moments. Patience is a tremendous virtue, the ability to wait for God to act on our behalf. We will look at four aspects of Job's patience in this chapter and see the great benefits of this quality.

1. Job's patience was part of his righteousness (Job 1:1-5). Job was a "perfect and upright" man. He lived a life of virtue before God, and God brought great blessings to him because of this. He was one of the three most righteous men of the Old Testament, along with Noah and Daniel (Ezekiel 14:14). His patience was an integral part of this righteousness. If we are going to live in righteousness, patience is an essential quality for us to have.

2. Job's patience overcame his trial (Job 1:6-2:13). Satan accused Job before God. He told God that Job only served him because of the blessings, not because he loved God. God allowed Satan to test Job. In one day all of Job's riches were lost, and his sons and daughters died. After Job remained faithful to God, Satan then compounded matters by placing painful boils all over Job's body. In a short time he had gone from being rich, healthy, and surrounded by a lovely family to being poor, sick, and alone. Even Job's wife told him to curse God and die (short break for a bit of marriage counseling; never give this instruction to your spouse!). Still, Job did not turn away from God, but blessed the name of the Lord. This was only possible because of his patience. When we go through trials, let's have patience and allow God to bring deliverance.

3. Job's patience enabled him to make a covenant with his eyes (Job 31:1-40). Job made a covenant with his eyes, that he would not lust after women. He would not even look at them, but had a heart of complete purity. He was patient even in this area, only having desire towards his wife and no other. In this media-saturated age where we are bombarded by immoral images, we also need to make a covenant with our eyes that we will stay pure before God.

4. Job's patience rewarded him with a double portion (Job 42:1-17). Job stayed faithful to God throughout his trial. At times he questioned God, but he never turned away. At the end of the trial, God rewarded Job for his faithfulness and gave him a double portion of blessing! All the riches he had were returned double, and he had many more sons and daughters. If we remain faithful and patient through trials, God will surely give deliverance and reward us as well.

Patience is a highly sought after but rarely found quality. Let's ask God to work this fruit of the Spirit into our lives that we may be strong as Job was.

CHAPTER 15: SAUL - INSECURITY
(1 SAMUEL 8-31)

I'm standing on the MRT (subway car) when it begins to move forward. I haven't taken the time to grab hold of the railings or loops in order to balance. Because of that, I start moving forward with the MRT. I bump into the person next to me before catching my balance and standing upright once again. It's a very embarrassing situation (especially when you're a big person and everyone on the train can see you!), and it all happened because I was in an insecure position. I am never secure on the train without holding on!

It's important in our spiritual lives to have security. We need to know that we are standing on a firm foundation in God, and that if God has called us, He is on our side and will overcome our weaknesses. Saul, the first king of Israel, was a man who never found that security in his life. He always considered himself unfit for the task God had called him to, and never learned to trust in God instead of focusing on his own inabilities. Because of this, his life and reign were a failure. We can learn four dangers of insecurity by studying the life of Saul.

1. Insecurity led the people to choose Saul as king (1 Samuel 8:1-12:25). After taking the Promised Land, the Israelites had been ruled by judges for around 400 years. The people of Israel decided they wanted to be like the nations around them and asked for a king. They were not secure in being God's people but wanted a man to follow, like everyone else had. This insecurity led God to give them Saul as king, a man who was also insecure. Don't seek security in the things unbelievers find it in - money, education, popularity, etc. - but find your security in God.

2. Insecurity led Saul to value people's approval more than God's (1 Samuel 13:1-15:35). Saul began to have problems soon into his reign as king. Once, he lost patience while waiting for the prophet Samuel and unlawfully sacrificed an offering by himself. Another time, he disobeyed God by not completely destroying the Amalekites; he kept the best of them alive. After Samuel confronted him with this sin, Saul begged Samuel to stay and still honor him before the people. Saul did not care that he had offended God, but he was so insecure he needed to look good in front of the people. We must always value God's approval above all else; our life is for Him and none other.

3. Insecurity led Saul to be jealous of David (1 Samuel 17:1-27:12). After Saul's sins, God chose David to be the next king and anointed him greatly. After David rescued Israel by killing the giant Goliath (a battle Saul was afraid to fight), Saul grew jealous of David's popularity. He then spent the next ten years of his life chasing David, trying to kill him. Ask God to rid all jealousy out of your heart and life. Realize that God is not comparing you to others, so you do not need to compare either. Jealousy is a terrible sin that can destroy us.

4. Insecurity led Saul to end his life in disaster (1 Samuel 28:1-31:13). At the end of his life, Saul lost all confidence in his relationship with God and went to a witch for counsel. He then went to battle, where he was defeated by the Philistines. Rather than allowing himself to die in the battle, he committed suicide. He could not trust in God but saw only his own failures. We must place our confidence in God and realize that He is the one fighting our battles.

Let's be secure in our relationship with Christ. Recognize that your security comes not from your self-worth but through Jesus; as we are connected to Him, we are safe from all danger and evil. Trust in Him and all other aspects of your life will come into right alignment.

CHAPTER 16: DAVID (PART 1) - YOUTH AFTER GOD (1 SAMUEL 16-17)

Have you ever heard a story about a child protégé? Maybe it was about a ten-year-old who had graduated from college. Or perhaps the six-year-old who could play all the works of Beethoven. It could have even been about a thirteen-year-old heart surgeon. These examples are very rare, but there is good news; God is looking to raise up many young protégés to do awesome things in the spirit. And we qualify not based on our natural intelligence but on our level of surrender to God.

David is a man who served God wholeheartedly from the time of his youth and is a tremendous example for all young people to follow. He is one of the most-loved characters in the Bible, and his story is so important that we will study him for the next three chapters. God called David "a man after God's heart" when David was still in his teens. In this chapter, we will look at four aspects of David's life as a young person, seeing how we also can be a youth after God.

1. David was faithful in small tasks (1 Samuel 16:1-11). David was the youngest son of his father Jesse, who had eight sons. As the youngest, it was his responsibility to watch his father's sheep. When Samuel came to anoint one of Jesse's sons as the next king, David faithfully continued working, although it was not an exciting task. He even risked his life for the sheep, killing a lion and a bear when they were attacking. Before God promotes us to great things, He is watching to see if we are faithful in the little things.

2. David was noticed by God (1 Samuel 16:12-13). Jesse called seven of his eight sons to meet the prophet Samuel, ignoring David. Nobody thought that little David could be chosen as the next king, but God noticed David's faithfulness and heart for Him. When everyone else was looking at the oldest, the biggest, and the strongest, God chose David to be the next king of Israel. Remember that God notices the little things that you do for Him. Do not seek the approval and recognition of man, but seek the approval of God, even in your every day tasks.

3. David had the anointing (1 Samuel 16:14-23). David had such an anointing on his life that when he played the harp, evil spirits had to flee. The servants of King Saul noticed this and brought David to play for Saul whenever he was troubled. David brought great relief to Saul, and was promoted to become Saul's armor bearer. David had an anointing and an excellent spirit that caused him to do great things at a young age. Press in to God and ask Him to anoint you in such a way that the enemy cannot stand before you.

4. David had faith to slay the giant (1 Samuel 17:1-58). The Israelites were at war with the Philistines, and the Philistine giant, Goliath, would taunt the Israelites daily. All of the warriors of Israel were scared to fight Goliath, but David was not. He volunteered to go to the battle and told Goliath he was not afraid of him for God would give David the victory. Goliath scoffed at David, but not for long - David killed Goliath with one shot from his sling. While the mature soldiers and everyone else saw the giant as an impossible foe, David realized that God was on his side. Have faith that God can use you to do the extraordinary when your faith is in the Almighty God. We cannot defeat the enemy on our own, but through Christ we are always victorious!

Let's have the overcoming faith of young David and be champions in our generation. God can use us, regardless of our age, to make a great impact in His Kingdom.

CHAPTER 17: DAVID (PART 2) - VICTORIOUS KING (1 SAMUEL 18-2 SAMUEL 10)

My team huddles together in the locker room, waiting for our coach's instructions before going out to play the game. "Remember guys, we have to run our offense. Keep the ball moving and cut to the lane. Play hard on defense; don't give them any three pointers. And if #25 gets the ball, put a double team on him right away! If you do these things, we will win this game!" Our coach has just given us our "keys to victory", and we run out of the locker room, ready to conquer!

There are also keys to victory in our spiritual lives. God desires each and every believer to be an overcoming champion through Christ! This chapter is the second in our study of David, and we will focus on the great victories that God gave him. David conquered enemy after enemy because of his faith in God. Four keys to his victory are listed below.

1. David's victories came through refusing to take revenge (1 Samuel 18:1-29:11).
After defeating Goliath, David became a mighty warrior for Israel. He grew so popular that Israel's king, Saul, grew extremely jealous of him, to the point of trying to kill David. David spent the next ten years running for his life from wicked King Saul. Twice during this period, David had the opportunity to kill Saul while Saul was unaware; both times, he declined. He refused to take vengeance into his own hands but waited for God. If we are going to be victorious in our Christian walk, we must not take revenge against those who harm us. Even if you have been mistreated, wait for God's vengeance and do not rejoice when your enemies are hurt.

2. David's victories came by encouraging himself in God (1 Samuel 30:1-2 Samuel 4:12). After 10 years of running from Saul, David and his men finally built one small camp called Ziklag. However, this camp was completely destroyed and their families kidnapped one day while they were gone. His own men then spoke of killing David. David's response is incredible - he encouraged himself in God! When everything looked horrible on the outside, David found strength by looking to God. Just three days later, God entirely turned the situation around, and David became king! It is absolutely vital that we learn to trust in God, even during our difficult times. Victory comes through trust in Him!

3. David's victories came to the taking of Zion (2 Samuel 5:1-25). Seven years after becoming king of Judah, David became king of all Israel. His first goal as king was to take possession of Mt. Zion. David's men destroyed the evil Jebusites, who had been controlling Zion for generations, and won the battle. David established Zion as the center of his kingdom. Zion is God's favorite place, and He also calls us to go to spiritual Mt. Zion. Let us make this pursuit a top priority as David did.

4. David's victories came in his passionate worship (2 Samuel 6:1-10:19). David was not just a warrior, he was a worshipper. He brought the Ark of the Covenant (which contained the presence and power of God) to Mt. Zion and passionately worshipped God there. David's passion was so great that God allowed the Israelites to worship before the ark without a veil. David was willing to become undignified before God. God is still looking for passionate, undignified worship today. Will you be that kind of worshipper? Your victories will come.

We are all called to be kings and priests of God (Revelation 5:10) and He wants us to be victorious. The Lord of all the universe is on our side; who can stand against us (Romans 8:31)? Go forth in His will as David did, and you will always be victorious.

CHAPTER 18: DAVID (PART 3) - RESTORATION (2 SAMUEL 11-24)

The late summer of 1942 was the lowest point of World War II for the Allies. Nation after nation (including France, the Philippines, and Singapore) had fallen before the seemingly invincible onslaught of the enemy. Resistance seemed futile and many feared the whole world was on the brink of German and Japanese control. However, the troops kept fighting, and within three years the Allies had claimed victory. They were restored from a place of defeat to one of great strength.

Restoration is an exciting process where our loss is turned into victory, our depression turned into joy, our weakness turned into strength, and our sin turned into righteousness. And the good news for us is, God specializes in restoration. If we are going through dark experiences or have painful times in our past, we can have faith that God can restore those areas. King David experienced God as a Restorer, and from his life we can learn four things about restoration.

1) Restoration can come to those who have committed horrific sin (2 Samuel 11:1-27). Despite being a man after God's heart, David had areas of sin in his life with which he had never dealt. One day when he should have been at war, he stayed at home and noticed a woman, Bathsheba, bathing on her rooftop. He ended up committing adultery with her and then compounded his sin by murdering her husband, Uriah. He was attempting to cover up his sin. This shows us that we must always cry out to God for a pure heart and ask Him to take all lust and immorality out of us. Even if we have been a Christian for a long time, we must always be vigilant against sin.

2) Restoration comes to those whose hearts are after God (2 Samuel 12:1-31). When David was confronted with his sin by the prophet Nathan, he confessed and cried out to God (Psalm 51). He realized his sin was primarily against God and humbly repented. His top concern was restoring his relationship with God; he did not care about his position or reputation. God brings restoration to those who confess their sins and love Him above all else. Don't be like Saul, who worried about the people when caught in his sin; be like David, who was concerned only with God.

3) Restoration comes to the patient (2 Samuel 13:1-20:26). After David's sin, several judgments took place upon him and his family. Although God had forgiven and restored him, sin still always has negative consequences; this is one reason it's better not to sin in the first place than to be restored! If David had complained and grown bitter, the restoration would have stopped but he accepted God's dealings. Learn to be patient when you are going through trials, particularly when the difficulty has been brought about by your own sin. God will grant deliverance in time.

4) Restoration is glorious (2 Samuel 21:1-24:25). At the end of David's life, he entered into a greater relationship with God than he had at the beginning. He passed great wisdom to Solomon, as well as all the materials that would be needed for the temple. His last words were filled with faith and vision. Moreover, Scripture tells us that in the Millennium David will rule as the prince of Jerusalem. He will be a restored king ruling a restored nation. God is a God of restoration-allow Him to restore any dead areas in your life!

In these three chapters we have seen just a glimpse of David's extraordinary life. He is an inspiring example of what God can do through one whose life is surrendered to Him. God is still looking today for people like this; young men and fathers; grandmothers and school girls; experienced and inexperienced. Will you be a David? May we say, "Yes!"

CHAPTER 19: SOLOMON - WISDOM (1 KINGS 1-11)

In life, we are known for many things. When I played basketball, I used to be known for my rebounding. As I grew older, I became known for my low post scoring. However, I've surely never been known for my shooting or ball handling skills! On the foosball table, I was known for my hard shot from my defensemen; when typing, I am known for the loud noise I make on the keyboard. What are you known for?

In this chapter we are studying Solomon (the son of David), a man who is known for one primary quality in his life. That quality is wisdom. Wisdom is the ability to make the right choices, and Solomon was granted tremendous wisdom from God. Wisdom is an absolute necessity in our time as well. We can learn much about wisdom through Solomon's life, including the following four qualities.

1. Wisdom must be desired (1 Kings 1:1-3:28). Solomon was made king after the death of his father, David. One night, near the beginning of Solomon's reign as king, God appeared to him in a dream and asked him what he desired. Solomon asked God for a wise and understanding heart. He knew that wisdom was the most important quality a ruler could have, greater than riches or honor or a long life. This truth had been taught to Solomon by his parents from a young age (Proverbs 1-9). We must likewise have a great desire for wisdom and cry out to God for it. If we ask God for wisdom, He will supply it liberally (James 1:6).

2. Wisdom builds God's house (1 Kings 4:1-8:66). The greatest achievement of Solomon's reign was the building of the beautiful temple for God. The temple was the most outstanding building on earth and was excellent in every way. Solomon's wisdom enabled him to build this amazing dwelling place. God wants us to build and to be His spiritual dwelling places, and it takes wisdom to do so.

3. Wisdom causes people to seek us out (1 Kings 9:1-10:13). Solomon's wisdom caused him to be the most respected and feared king in all the earth. Rulers from around the world would come to hear his wisdom, including the queen of Sheba, who came with a great many gifts. If we have the wisdom of God, people in the world will come to us for advice. Wisdom opens many doors for us to teach people the ways of God and effect positive change in our society.

4. Wisdom must be combined with righteousness (1 Kings 10:14-11:43). As a young man, Solomon loved God and walked in his ways, but he became backslidden as he grew older. He committed great immorality and disobeyed God's commandments to the kings. His many wives even convinced him to worship their gods, and he built idols all over the holy city of Jerusalem. This God-fearing, wisdom-seeking young man who started out so well ended his life as an idol-worshipping, hardhearted, backslidden king. Although Solomon had wisdom (he knew the right choices), he did not have righteousness (doing the right choices). Wisdom is something we must seek and desire with all of our hearts, but it is imperative that it is mixed with righteousness. Just being in church for many years and hearing and knowing what is right is not enough; we must then do what's right.

Let's follow young Solomon's example in seeking wisdom, but then on top of that let's ask God to put to death our old nature and make us righteous as well. Wisdom and righteousness should be the hallmarks of our lives!

CHAPTER 20: REHOBOAM - WRONG CHOICES (2 CHRONICLES 10-12)

Which shirt should I wear today, the blue and white long sleeved or the red tee? What cereal do I want to eat for breakfast? Should I walk or take the bus? Every day we are confronted with literally thousands of choices. Most of these choices are insignificant, but some carry the utmost importance! The choices we make determine our destiny, both in this life and in eternity.

Rehoboam was the son of Solomon, living about 900 years before the time of Christ. His life and kingdom were ruined through the foolish choices that he made. Studying his negative example is beneficial for us, as we can see what behaviors we must avoid if we are to live a victorious Christian life. There are at least four warnings from Rehoboam's life of which we should take note.

1. Rehoboam made a wrong choice in not obeying wise counsel (2 Chronicles 10:1-15). Shortly after he became king, the people of Israel came to Rehoboam to ask him to demand less of them than Solomon had. Rehoboam counseled with the older men about how he should respond, and the old men told him to give a kind answer. However, Rehoboam's young friends told him to threaten the people that he would be even tougher than his father. Rehoboam listened to his friends and spoke roughly to the people. He ignored the wise counsel of the experienced and listened to his foolish friends. Learn to look for counsel in those who have wisdom, and obey wise counsel when it is received. Do not ignore the voice of experience but treasure those who have walked before you.

2. Rehoboam's wrong choice led to him losing the kingdom (2 Chronicles 10:16-11:17). After his rough answer, the people of Israel (led by Jeroboam) rebelled against Rehoboam's leadership. Eleven of the twelve tribes followed Jeroboam, leaving only the tribe of Judah under Rehoboam's control and splitting the nation in two. As the grandson of David, it was Rehoboam's destiny to rule all of Israel, but his wrong choice caused him to lose most of his inheritance. God has placed a great call on each of our lives, but we must make the right choices in order to inherit all that He has for us.

3. Rehoboam made a wrong choice by not learning from his father's mistakes (2 Chronicles 11:18-23). Solomon's great sin was lust and immorality, leading him to have many ungodly wives and leaving him in a terrible condition. Rehoboam did not learn from his father's weakness and made the exact same mistake. He was also consumed by lust and disobeyed God by having many wives. Don't repeat the mistakes of those who have gone before you but learn from them. Ask God to remove all lust and immorality from your life.

4. Rehoboam made a wrong choice in forsaking God when he was strong (2 Chronicles 12:1-16). There was a brief time in his reign over Judah where Rehoboam did obey God. As a result God began to bless and strengthen the kingdom. However, Rehoboam responded to God's blessings by turning away. He trusted in his own strength and ended up being judged. The king of Egypt came and stole many treasures from Judah. Rehoboam had a very sad end. When God makes you strong, keep trusting in Him and never look to your own strength.

Ask God to always cause you to make the right choices so you do not follow the mistakes of this king. Rehoboam could have had so much but ended his life in disappointment because he made choices out of his own heart and not in the wisdom of God.

CHAPTER 21: AHAB - SOLD OUT TO EVIL (1 KINGS 16-22)

What's the worst grade you've ever gotten on a test? I remember a math course (MTH 012) I took during my first semester at Oakland University. I was shocked by my poor grade on one of the exams! At the end of the semester, I ended up with the lowest score I had ever received on a report card. Without doubt, my performance in that class was the worst I have ever had in school.

We are going to study the worst king in the history of Israel, Ahab. The Scriptures tell us that he was the most evil man to ever rule God's people, selling himself to work wickedness in God's eyes. This terrible man brought devastation upon the nations of Israel and Judah. It is important for us to study him because Ahab was not an ignorant heathen but rather someone who knew who God was and knew God's commandments and deliberately chose to disobey Him. Likewise, many of us know the ways of God and must be sure that we do not follow his evil example, four parts of which we will look at in this chapter.

1. Ahab led the people in the worship of Baal (1 Kings 16:28-18:46). Ahab introduced the worship of Baal to the nation of Israel. He set up many altars and groves to this false god, ushering in a great increase of idolatry and immorality in the nation. He did not stop leading the people in the worship of Baal even though God greatly judged the nation. His evil actions brought great suffering to those under him. Make sure that you do not worship the idols of our age (sexual immorality, materialism, etc.). Idolatry always leads to destruction; ask God to give you a pure heart that worships only Him.

2. Ahab was led to even greater evil by his wife Jezebel (1 Kings 19:1-20:43). Ahab's wickedness was compounded by his extraordinarily evil wife, Jezebel. His decision to marry her led him into all kinds of mistakes. She was responsible for trying to kill the great prophet Elijah. Even if Ahab had wanted to do right, it would have been extremely difficult because of his wife. Do not make close friendships with sinful people, for they will drag you into sin. Be especially careful in the area of romantic relationships; as a Christian, you must never consider being involved with an unbeliever. You will not influence them for righteousness, but they will always influence you for evil, as Jezebel did.

3. Ahab coveted things that did not belong to him (1 Kings 21:1-29). Although Ahab was the richest man in the kingdom, he was not satisfied with what he had and wanted a vineyard that belonged to another man, Naboth. He was obsessed with this piece of land and coveted it. When Naboth refused to sell it to Ahab, he was so depressed that Jezebel arranged for Naboth to be killed so Ahab could possess it. His covetousness led to murder. Don't long after material things, and don't desire to be rich. Be satisfied with what God has given you, and guard your heart against covetousness.

4. Ahab did not respect the Word of the Lord (1 Kings 22:1-40). Ahab was warned by the prophet Micaiah not to go to battle against Syria. He disobeyed this warning, as he had disobeyed countless others in his life. This time his disobedience cost him his life as he died in the battle. His life ended in a disastrous, sinful state, with his nation defeated.

Ahab's children continued to carry on his sinful legacy, in the end bringing irreparable harm to Israel and serious judgments on Judah. Today, Ahab's name is universally associated with evil and cruelty. Cultivate a lifestyle of obeying God's Word, and you will not end up like Ahab. Righteousness and true success in life come through hearing and obeying God's instructions.

CHAPTER 22: ELIJAH - FIRE OF GOD
(1 KINGS 17-2 KINGS 2)

Everybody likes a good campfire. In my 29 years of existence, I have been to too many youth camps to count, and the part of the camp that everyone looks forward to the most is always the campfire! And while we are at the campfire, everyone relaxes and has a great time. Some people are roasting marshmallows; others are singing songs; someone else is telling a funny story. The fire always draws the people!

Just as fire is important in the natural, so it is in the spiritual; God wants His fire to be burning inside of each one of us. The fire of God is the consuming passion for His presence and zeal to win the lost that overtake and envelop us. It is Spirit-given, Spirit-breathed, and Spirit-inspired. Elijah was an Old Testament prophet who lived about 800 years before the coming of Christ and his life is an excellent example of the fire of God in action. This chapter we will look at four things we can learn about the fire of God from studying his life.

1. *The fire of God releases us into the miraculous (1 Kings 17:1-24).* The miraculous anointing on Elijah's life was perhaps greater than that of any prophet before him. As a judgment upon backslidden Israel and their wicked king Ahab, Elijah prayed and God stopped rain from falling on the land for seven years. God miraculously provided food and drink for Elijah during this time. Elijah also raised a young boy from the dead. He was a man full of the fire and miracles of God. Burning with passion for God and His Kingdom is a key to receiving the anointing for miracles in our life as well.

2. *The fire of God reveals His salvation to others (1 Kings 18:1-46).* During Elijah's time, Israel was greatly backslidden and serving the false god Baal. Elijah gave the 450 prophets of Baal a challenge; they would sacrifice to Baal and Elijah to Jehovah. Whoever sent fire down upon the offering would be the true God of Israel. Baal's prophets accepted and cried out for fire throughout the day, but none ever came. Elijah then prepared his sacrifice and prayed for the fire. God responded by sending His fire down from heaven and consuming the sacrifice. When the people of Israel saw it, they fell on their faces and proclaimed that the Lord is God. If we live a sacrificial life of prayer and burn with holy fire, people will likewise see that Christ is the true Lord. A generation can be saved!

3. *The fire of God repels all of God's enemies (1 Kings 19:1-2 Kings 1:18).* Elijah's actions earned him many enemies. At one point Ahab sent his military to capture Elijah. However, the fire of God came down from heaven and burned up those coming to imprison him. Of course in the New Testament age in which we live, we do not desire to see fire kill people who oppose us, but we do need God's fire to drive away spiritual principalities and powers that oppose His will in our lives. God's fire goes before Him and burns up all His enemies! Ask God to send His fire to drive the enemy out of your life.

4. *The fire of God reproduces itself in others (1 Kings 2:1-2:25).* Elijah's servant was a man named Elisha. Elijah did not die as most men do, but because of his tremendous walk with God, was instead taken up to heaven in a chariot of fire. Elisha saw this happen and inherited a double portion of the

anointing that had been on Elijah's life. Elijah's fire was transmitted to Elisha. If you burn for God, it will not stay contained within you; fire always spreads. You can be the spark that starts an outbreak in your home, your cell group, your church, your school, your workplace, and even your nation!

God is looking for firebrands who will carry His fire to the world. Will you be one of them? Let's burn for God!

CHAPTER 23: ELISHA - THE ANOINTING (2 KINGS 2-13)

In my senior year in high school, I was the captain of our school basketball team, the Mt. Zion Eagles. I had spent the previous two years studying our previous captain, a friend of mine whose basketball skills I had long admired. I knew that I was going to be his successor, and I wanted to do my best to follow well in his footsteps.

Today we're going to look at the prophet Elisha, a man who also followed in someone else's footsteps. He was the servant of the mighty prophet Elijah, and followed him up to the point where Elijah was taken up into heaven. Elisha received a double portion of the anointing that was on Elijah's life, and his life is a powerful example of what the anointing of God can accomplish. The anointing is the enabling of the Holy Spirit to do the works of God, and we can learn the following four things about the anointing from Elisha's miracle-filled life.

1. The anointing comes through persistence (2 Kings 2:1-3:27). Elisha had followed Elijah as his servant for many years before it was time for Elijah to be taken up into heaven. As Elijah was preparing for God to take him, he discouraged Elisha from following him further. It was a test to see if Elisha really was committed to God. Elisha steadfastly refused to turn away from Elijah, and stayed right beside him until Elijah was taken up into heaven. Because of his persistence, God rewarded Elisha with a double portion of Elijah's anointing. If you want the anointing of God in your life, you must never give up but hold on to God in prayer, asking for more of Him in your life.

2. The anointing increases with expectation (2 Kings 4:1-4:7). One of the prophets under Elisha died and left his wife and two sons in deep debt. The woman cried out to Elisha for a miracle of provision. She had only one pot of oil left in her possession, but Elisha instructed her to borrow many vessels from her neighbors. After she did so, the oil from the one pot was poured into the many different pots and miraculously filled every one! It did not stop flowing until there were no more empty pots. Oil is a type of the anointing of the Holy Spirit, and this miracle shows us that the more we expect God to fill us, the more He will be able to fill us. His anointing is infinite, and the Holy Spirit in us is limited only by our own low expectation and faith. Believe and expect God for great things, and they will happen.

3. The anointing brings life to the dead (2 Kings 4:8-44). A barren woman became a follower of Elisha. God promised the woman a son through Elisha, and the son was born. After several years, the boy suddenly died. The woman called for Elisha, and after Elisha stretched himself upon the boy and called out to God, the child came back to life. Elisha worked several extraordinary miracles in his life. When the anointing fills your life, you also will be able to bring life to the spiritually dead around you.

4. The anointing works in mysterious ways (2 Kings 5:1-13:25). A nobleman from Syria named Naaman came to Elisha to ask for healing from his leprosy. Elisha instructed Naaman to wash in the filthy Jordan River seven times. At first Naaman was horrified, reasoning that there were several rivers nicer than the Jordan in his home country of Syria. After his servants reasoned with him, however, Naaman obeyed, and he was completely healed of his horrible disease. Several of Elisha's miracles functioned in ways that did not make sense to the logical, rational mind. If we want the anointing of God to function in our lives, we may have to do things that don't always make sense. Obey whatever God tells you, and you will open the door for the anointing!

We often sing songs about the anointing and hear messages about it, but God doesn't want it to stop there; He wants us to actually be anointed. Let's press in to God and ask for this wonderful gift.

CHAPTER 24: JEHOSHAPHAT - WRONG FRIENDSHIPS (2 CHRONICLES 17-20)

I remember once when my cousin and I were in an impromptu wrestling match against two of our other friends (it was many years ago and we were wrestling just for fun). I was flying around the room, trying to knock down our opponents, while he was taking it easy. I jumped off a mattress when, to my horror, the man I was about to knock over moved out of the way. Now, my cousin was directly in my path. I could have pulled up and not hit him, but I had so much momentum it seemed it would be a waste to not drive into somebody. So I put my shoulder down and knocked my teammate and cousin to the ground. At that moment, I think we both realized we had the wrong teammate and the alliance ended for that match!

In our spiritual lives, making the right alliances is vitally important. Jehoshaphat is a prime example of this truth. He was a righteous man and king of Judah whose life was ultimately unsuccessful because of the foolish choices he made in his relationships. It's not enough to do what is right on your own, you must surround yourselves with others who do what is right. Four lessons about wrong friendships can be learned from Jehoshaphat's life.

1. *Wrong friendships can be made by righteous people (2 Chronicles 17:1-19).* The first thing we must understand about Jehoshaphat is that, personally, he was a righteous man. He destroyed the idols that were in the land of Judah and had victory over many enemies. He possessed a true love for God and His Kingdom. Yet, being righteous on his own was not enough for him to live a victorious life. In your own life, being righteous is vital but wisdom is also needed.

2. *Wrong friendships lead us to make foolish decisions (2 Chronicles 18:1-34).* Jehoshaphat made an alliance with the wicked king of Israel, Ahab. They decided to go to war against Syria. A prophet warned them that the battle would end in disaster, but Jehoshaphat agreed to go with Ahab anyway. Ahab then convinced Jehoshaphat to wear his kingly robes to battle while Ahab went dressed as a common soldier. This was a ridiculous agreement as the Assyrian king had instructed his soldiers to only kill the king of Israel. Jehoshaphat was so blinded by his friendship to evil Ahab that he agreed to it. He survived the battle only through the mercy of God (while Ahab was killed by a stray arrow). Wrong friendships will also lead you to do foolish things, even when you should know better.

3. *Wrong friendships keep us from hating wickedness (2 Chronicles 19:1-11).* After the battle a prophet came and rebuked Jehoshaphat for loving and helping those who hate God. If we do not break out of wrong relationships we will never have a clear hatred for sin. It is not enough to love righteousness, God also wants us to hate wickedness. This applies to many areas in our lives - the music we listen to, the shows we watch, the friends we keep, the business deals we make, and many other things.

4. *Wrong friendships cause our works to be destroyed (2 Chronicles 20:1-37).* Even after this warning, Jehoshaphat continued his wrong relationships up till the end of his life. He joined Ahab's wicked son Ahaziah in a naval project, and all their ships were destroyed as a judgment. Despite his righteousness, Jehoshaphat left no godly legacy or inheritance because of his wicked relationships.

Let's ask God to give us wisdom that we make right friendships throughout our lives. That way we can make a lasting impact in our world.

CHAPTER 25: JEHU - ZEALOUS PRIDE (2 KINGS 9-10)

Have you ever been in a rush to get somewhere? I must admit that when I was younger, I used to drive in a hurry. Quite often, I would exceed the speed limit, cut in and out of lanes, do anything to arrive at my destination just a little bit sooner. Such behavior was dangerous, but I unwisely did it because I always liked to get places fast. Many of you have probably also felt the need to speed!

Jehu is a Biblical figure who was always in a hurry; in fact, he was known for his furious chariot driving! God raised up Jehu to deal with the huge problem of Baal worship after the wicked influence of Ahab, Jezebel, and their children. Jehu accomplished much for God and had a great zeal to accomplish it, and in this area is a good example for us. However, at the root of his zeal was not love for God but rather, his own pride. Thus, his life also serves as a warning, that zeal alone is not sufficient; we must have righteous life. We will look at four aspects of his life.

1. Jehu had the anointing and call of God (2 Kings 9:1-13). The prophet Elisha sent one of his servants to anoint Jehu as the next king over Israel. He was to replace Joram, the wicked son of Ahab. Jehu had a real call and empowerment from God to bring down this evil family. He was a vessel of God's wrath against Ahab. We see from this that it's possible to have the anointing of God and do good things for Him and yet never be approved by Him. Don't be satisfied merely with God's call and anointing but press in for His righteousness.

2. Jehu was impatient (2 Kings 9:14-20). When Jehu was coming to attack the tower that King Joram was in, he was spotted by a watchman. The watchman knew it was Jehu coming because of the reckless way he drove his chariot. Jehu was always in a rush and moved with no patience. In our own lives, it's important to ask God for the fruit of patience. Don't rush into God's call but allow Him to promote and use you at the right time.

3. Jehu destroyed the enemies of God (2 Kings 9:21-10:28). Jehu's zeal led him to do many great works for God. First he killed the two evil kings, Joram of Israel and Ahaziah of Judah (they were both descendants of Ahab). He then brought the promised judgment against Jezebel, ordering her to be thrown out of the window to her death, and leaving her dead body for the dogs. He went on to kill all of Ahab's descendants and eventually tricked all the worshippers of Baal in the nation to come together, and he killed them all. Jehu was a powerful instrument of God's judgment and even bragged of his zeal to others. He cleansed the land of the worship of Baal. He had an admirable passion to rid the land of evil worship.

4. Jehu never allowed God to deal with his own life (2 Kings 10:29-36). Though Jehu destroyed Baal, he never truly worshipped God in his own life. He hated the sins of Ahab but didn't love the ways of God. We must not judge the sins of others when we have not dealt with our own. It's not enough to merely have zeal on Sundays or to be excited during prayer meeting if we neglect our own lives. Having zeal is a definite necessity, but we must also stay humble before God if we want to receive an everlasting reward from Him.

God is looking for zealous, righteous *and* humble servants. Though there are many positive aspects to Jehu's life, in the end he was considered a failure as the Bible tells us he did not walk in the ways of God. If you are zealous, hold on to that zeal and ask God to increase it, but also ask Him to give you a wise, righteous, and humble heart.

CHAPTER 26: UZZIAH - HELP FROM GOD (2 CHRONICLES 26)

Several years ago when I was going to Bible school in upstate New York, I was driving back to school after a night out with my friends. As I exited the empty freeway, I heard a terrible noise, "CRUNK, CRunk, crunk..."; it was the noise of my car breaking down. My friends and I were stranded on the side of the road. The school's maintenance man ended up coming to help us. He towed my car the remaining two miles. We were all very happy to receive the help!

We have all been in situations where we needed help. In our spiritual lives, we are actually constantly in need of God's aid. Uzziah was a king of Judah whose name means "strength of the Lord". And in the first portion of Uzziah's reign, God did greatly help him. In the end, however, Uzziah turned himself away from God's aid. We can learn several lessons about God's help from the life of Uzziah, four of which we will examine here.

1. God's help enables us to be righteous (2 Chronicles 26:1-5). Uzziah was known for doing what was right in the eyes of God. His righteousness was recognized by the people in his nation as he followed the advice of the godly priest, Zechariah. If we are going to be righteous in our day, we also must rely on the grace and help of God. He not only commands us to be righteous, He also offers us the ability to do so.

2. God's help gives us victory in battles (2 Chronicles 26:6-15). Uzziah also brought great military victories to Israel. He built strong towers and destroyed the enemies of God. Surrounding nations served Israel and gave presents because of their fear of Uzziah. The Lord "marvelously helped" him in battle, and his every victory was credited to God. We are also called to fight spiritual battles against sin, principalities, and wickedness. If we trust in God and faithfully follow Him, He will always help and give us the victory.

3. God's help should not lead us to arrogance (2 Chronicles 26:16-19). The great tragedy of Uzziah's life was that after God had greatly helped him, he became proud and arrogant. After God had made him strong, his heart became lifted up in his own might and he began considering himself to be someone great. He disobeyed God's law by acting as a priest, and disobeyed the priests who tried to stop him from making this mistake. This arrogance is also a great danger in our lives. When God gives us victories and success, let's always point the glory back to Him. We must always realize that we are nothing without His help and thus remain humble at all times.

4. God's help should not be presumed (2 Chronicles 26:20-23). As a punishment for trying to do the job of a priest, Uzziah was plagued with leprosy. He lived as a leper in a separate house for the rest of his life, not even being allowed into the temple. He finally died of the disease. He was never healed as his heart had turned away from God. We cannot assume that because God has helped us in the past He will help us in the future.

Our hearts must always be humble before Him to invite His aid. He is looking to help you in your everyday life, but you must accept His help. Let's follow the example of Uzziah in his early life and allow God to make us strong.

CHAPTER 27: HEZEKIAH - COMPLETE TRUST (2 KINGS 18-20)

Have you ever worried about whether or not gravity was going to work? As in, you're walking down the street one day and you begin to think, "Wow, I hope I don't float off into the sky. I really hope gravity works today!" When you drop something, do you wonder if it's really going to fall? If you are a sane person, you have answered "no" to these questions! We don't question gravity; we trust it completely.

Our trust in God should be no less than our trust in gravity or anything else. Hezekiah was a king of Judah whose life exemplifies complete, implicit trust in God. He trusted in God more than any king, before or after him (2 Kings 18:5), and as such his life is a powerful example to us. Trust in God is having faith in Him to always bring about His perfect purposes in our lives and not doubting His ways. Hezekiah's complete trust in God brought about at least four blessings in his life.

1. Hezekiah's trust caused him to cleave to God (2 Kings 18:1-7). God's Word tells us that Hezekiah "clave" unto God. This means he stayed as close to God as possible, like a little child clinging to his mother. He lived a life of righteousness and holiness because he trusted that God's ways were better than his own. He drew near to God as he had complete faith that knowing God was more important than anything else. In order for us to draw near and be a friend of God, we first need to trust that He is good and is in control of every situation.

2. Hezekiah's trust caused him to turn to God in time of desperate need (2 Kings 18:8-19:19). The king of Assyria had just destroyed the nation of Israel and now was surrounding Jerusalem, Hezekiah's capital city. The Assyrians had more than one hundred thousand soldiers, while Judah didn't even have two thousand. The situation was absolutely hopeless and surrender was the only logical solution. However, Hezekiah turned to God in this moment of deepest need. Instead of surrendering, he called for the priests and prophets and sought God. He acknowledged that Assyria did have a powerful army, but that God was more powerful. When you are faced with impossible situations, turn to God as Hezekiah did, and not to human wisdom.

3. Hezekiah's trust caused him to be victorious over his dreadful enemy (2 Kings 19:20-37). God heard Hezekiah's prayers and declared through the prophet, Isaiah, that he would cause Judah to be victorious. During the night, the angel of the Lord went through the camp of Assyrians and killed one hundred and eighty-five thousand of their soldiers. The king quickly retreated and ended up being killed by his own two sons. God had delivered Judah from sure destruction. No matter how powerful the enemy that is facing you, trusting in God will always lead to your victory.

4. Hezekiah's trust caused him to be healed (2 Kings 20:1-21). Shortly before this battle with Assyria, Hezekiah became deathly ill. He pleaded with God for healing and God sent Isaiah to confirm that he would be healed. As a sign of the healing, the sun moved backwards ten degrees in a truly remarkable miracle. Hezekiah lived for another fifteen years in health, as he wisely trusted God before he trusted doctors. We serve a God of healing and miracles; trust him for health for you and your family members.

God delivers those who trust in Him. What promises has He made to you? Trust in Him and you will never be disappointed.

CHAPTER 28: JONAH - MERCY OF GOD (JONAH 1-4)

What is the biggest fish that you have ever seen? I remember a time when my friends and I were on vacation and we decided to rent wave runners to motor around in the Atlantic Ocean. As we were riding, we were amazed to see dolphins surround our wave runners and start to swim alongside us. No matter how fast we made our boats go, the dolphins could keep us with us. It was truly impressive to see these amazing creatures up close.

In this chapter we will be studying the prophet Jonah, a man who saw a very big fish much closer than we would ever want to see one! Jonah, of course, was actually swallowed by the great fish when he disobeyed God and refused to preach to the city of Nineveh. However, the story does not end there but God restored Jonah and brought about His purposes through him. The theme of Jonah's life is the mercy of God, and that great mercy can be clearly seen throughout his story. We will see four ways that God's mercy is displayed through the story of Jonah.

1. God's mercy is displayed in Jonah's disobedience (Jonah 1:1-17). The story of Jonah begins with God instructing Jonah to go to Nineveh and tell the people to repent. Nineveh, however, was the world's most wicked city. It would have been very dangerous for Jonah to go there and he did not want to preach God's word to that city. Jonah decided to run away from God and go in the opposite direction of Nineveh. God did not let Jonah run away for long and caused him to be swallowed by a great fish. Even this punishment clearly shows God's mercy. God did not let Jonah stay separated from Him but caused circumstances to come to Jonah that would lead him to repentance. Thank God for the times in your life where He used difficult situations to point you towards repentance. God's judgments upon His children are always meant to lead us back into proper relationship with Him.

2. God's mercy is displayed with Jonah's repentance (Jonah 2:1-10). After being in the belly of the fish for three days and three nights, Jonah cried out to God for repentance. God caused the fish to vomit Jonah back out onto dry land. God had great mercy on Jonah, the once disobedient prophet, by forgiving him and delivering him from his punishment. If you have sinned against God, realize that He will forgive you if you will sincerely repent for your wrongdoing. God is a God of the second chance, and He gave Jonah a second chance to go to Nineveh.

3. God's mercy is displayed by Jonah's preaching (Jonah 3:1-10). Jonah went to Nineveh after the second chance he was given. He preached to this extremely wicked city that they needed to repent. Amazingly, the people of Nineveh, all the way up to the king, believed Jonah and repented before God. The king even proclaimed a fast throughout the land that all the people followed. God saw Nineveh's repentance and decided not to destroy the city. This illustrates that God can be merciful to the worst of sinners. Never assume that someone is beyond the mercy of God. Even the biggest troublemaker can find repentance if he turns in faith to God.

4. God's mercy is displayed through Jonah's reaction (Jonah 4:1-11). Jonah, however, was displeased that God forgave the people of Nineveh. He had not yet understood the mercy of God and wanted

God to bring judgment on the city. God explained to Jonah that Nineveh was very important to Him and that Jonah should not be angry that God was merciful. This shows us that God is concerned with the lives of men and women everywhere. He does not desire any to perish but wants to bring salvation to all.

Always remember; God does not desire to destroy sinners but to save them! He is a merciful God and will save all who call out to Him. Thank God for His mercy, for that is the only reason we are saved. Let's rejoice in the mercy and grace of God, and love in a way that is reflective of what His mercy has done for us.

CHAPTER 29: ISAIAH - TRUE PROPHET (ISAIAH 1-66)

Have you ever made a bad prediction? Many people have. In 1977, Ken Olson, the founder of Digital Equipment Corp., said, "There is no reason anyone would ever want a computer in their home." A Western Union internal memo in 1876 declared, "The telephone has too many shortcomings to be seriously considered as a method of communication. The device is inherently of no value to us." The famed British scientist, Lord Kelvin, stated in 1899, "Radio has no future. Heavier-than-air flying machines are impossible. X-rays will prove to be a hoax." One year, I said that my favorite football team, the Detroit Lions, was actually going to win a championship. Those were some extraordinarily wrong statements!

Isaiah was a Biblical prophet who predicted the future, but he did it through the Spirit of God. Thus, not one of his prophecies failed. He was a man of revelation, seeing into the future with extraordinary accuracy. He was also a high-ranking member of society, yet had extreme sensitivity to the Spirit of God. His visions of Christ still minister to billions today. We will look at four qualities Isaiah possessed as a true prophet of God.

1. Isaiah was a prophet of vision (Isaiah 1:1-6:4). Throughout his ministry Isaiah had visions from God. The Lord gave him eyes to see into the spirit. The most extraordinary vision he had occurred in the year King Uzziah died, when he saw God high and lifted up on his throne. Isaiah was awed by the holiness of God and overwhelmed by the vision, changing his life forever. Let's press in to truly know God and ask Him to give us a revelation of his glory as well.

2. Isaiah was a prophet of humility (Isaiah 6:5-35:10). When Isaiah saw the Lord, he cried out in repentance. He was a godly man but still had the humility to see his sin in relation to God's perfection. Moreover, Isaiah did not hold on to the dignity of his high position in the king's court but was always obedient to God's instructions, even walking barefoot and without his clothes for three full years. We should likewise be willing to do whatever God asks us to do, never considering ourselves too good for His commands.

3. Isaiah was a prophet of power (Isaiah 36:1-39:8). Isaiah was also a man of great power. God used him to heal King Hezekiah of his deadly disease. He even prophesied that the sun would move backwards on the sundial as a sign of this healing. Moreover, he gave Hezekiah the promise from God that Israel's impossible enemy, the Assyrians, would be defeated. Numerous miracles took place in Isaiah's ministry. Let's ask God for the gifts of His Spirit, so that we also can flow in miracles and healings.

4. Isaiah was a prophet of the Gospel (Isaiah 40:1-66:24). Isaiah presented the truths of the Gospel more clearly than any other Old Testament prophet. Though he lived more than 700 years before the coming of Christ, he accurately prophesied of Christ's birth, ministry, death, resurrection, and ultimate triumph. He realized that the Messiah would have to suffer for the sins of man. He is known above all for his portrayal of Christ. May the same be said about us; that in all we do, we spread the message of the Gospel of Jesus. There is no greater message, so let's follow Isaiah's example and spread it to those all around us.

We live in a time when many do not have the word of the Lord and prophets are needed, but it is essential that we seek the Lord for purity and a true message, as Isaiah had. In the Bible, a true prophet is always known for the complete accuracy of his messages.

CHAPTER 30: JOSIAH - RADICAL DEVOTION (2 KINGS 22-23)

Ten years ago, I attended a memorable American football game at the 80,000 seat Pontiac Silverdome. My favorite team, the Detroit Lions, was trying to clinch a playoff spot and a sell-out crowd screamed nonstop for them to win. Even more, the Lion's best player (Barry Sanders) was going for an important statistical record. The passion and intensity of the crowd was mind-numbing. I'll never forget the noise of the 80,000 clamoring fans. It's amazing how completely passionate and devoted people can become for something as ultimately unimportant as a sporting event.

We should also live our lives with radical devotion, with a passion that is directed to an infinitely valuable Lord. Jesus is the reason we exist, and we should serve Him with all of our energy, time, and abilities. Josiah was a king of Judah who lived radically devoted to God. In fact, 2 Kings 23:25 tells us that he turned to God more than any other king before him (this even includes the great King David!). Josiah showed his passion in at least four ways we will examine.

1. Josiah burned with the fire of God (2 Kings 22:1-2). The name Josiah means "the fire of God." As his name indicated, Josiah did indeed burn with that holy fire through his intense righteousness. He had a passion for God and a zeal to spread the glory of His name. He did what was right without turning to the right hand or the left. Let's ask God to put His holy fire into our lives, that consuming passion for His presence and zeal to win the lost.

2. Josiah remembered the Law of God (2 Kings 22:3-20). The previous kings of Judah had ignored the Law of God, but Josiah recovered it. When he heard God's commandments, he led the nation in repentance and pledged his obedience to God. In our times, we are no longer under the Law but grace, yet God still has a holy standard He expects us to follow. Let us never throw off righteousness but seek to know and obey God's ways all of our days.

3. Josiah relentlessly tore up every idol (2 Kings 23:1-20). After reading the Law, Josiah dedicated himself to obliterating idolatry from the land of Judah. He destroyed every idol without mercy; burning them, stamping them, grinding them to powder. He was so zealous he even went into neighboring countries to tear down idols there. We must follow this example to rid idolatry completely from our lives. Don't let any small idol of materialism, lust, pride, or anything else remain in your heart but go to war against your fallen nature. Be like Josiah, and never rest until every idol is torn down.

4. Josiah celebrated salvation (2 Kings 23:21-30). The Passover was the Jewish feast celebrating their salvation from Egyptian bondage. For many generations the Israelites had not properly kept the feast, but Josiah re-instituted it and held the greatest Passover in the history of the nation. He remembered God's great goodness in their lives. Let's always celebrate the salvation God has given us and never forget that miracle He worked inside of us. We celebrate salvation by testifying of it to other believers, praising and worshipping God for it, and telling the unsaved the Good News.

Josiah lived life full speed for the Lord. His passion and devotion was not up and down, but had true substance and knowledge behind it. We should be challenged to be like Josiah, and live life with a radical passion for the One who has saved us.

CHAPTER 31: JEREMIAH - WEEPING PROPHET (JEREMIAH 1-LAMENTATIONS 5)

Have you ever seen a grown man cry? I remember one playoff basketball game a few years ago where one team lost and their superstar cried and cried after it was over. The thought of his season ending without a championship brought him to tears! This was quite amazing to see, as most men don't want to be seen crying very often.

Jeremiah is a man who is often known as "The Weeping Prophet." He had a soft heart towards God and compassion for the people. He lived about six hundred years before the time of Christ and knew that his nation, Judah, was in sin and deeply offending God. He realized the pain that this sin caused God and cried over the terrible judgment that was coming. His tears were truly great, as the same things that move God's heart moved his heart. He was only a young man when he started his ministry and was a great light to his nation, a true prophet who pointed the people towards God. This great man had at least four qualities that we should follow.

1. Jeremiah was called before birth (Jeremiah 1:1-19). God told Jeremiah that he had been chosen before he was even born (Jeremiah 1:5). God chose Jeremiah to be a prophet and knew him before he was even conceived! For this reason Jeremiah could be strong in the face of opposition and fear. It is important for us to realize that God's call on us came even before we were created. Thus our effectiveness is not a matter of our strength but God's strength. His thoughts towards us are great and we need to learn to simply obey Him with boldness.

2. Jeremiah had fire in his spirit (Jeremiah 2:1-20:9). The Word of God in Jeremiah was like a fire in his bones (Jeremiah 20:9). He burned with such a passion that he was not able to hold in the Word of God. The fiery message God had given him burned through the lies and bondages of the enemy. Ask God to fill you with a fire on the inside that can be felt when you speak. We should burn with the message of His righteousness and holiness.

3. Jeremiah was faithful through captivity (Jeremiah 20:10-52:34). Jeremiah was abused by the people many times for his righteous message. He was beaten, thrown into prison, and ignored. Yet he remained faithful to speak God's Word. Moreover, he encouraged the backslidden people to turn back to God and accept His judgment, which was captivity to Babylon. The people disobeyed and would not accept the captivity. We should learn from Jeremiah to always obey God, even through times of trial and difficulty.

4. Jeremiah proclaimed God's faithfulness (Lamentations 1:1-5:22). Jeremiah's faithfulness stemmed from his realization that God was always more faithful. In the midst of his many prophecies of judgment, he knew that one day God would restore His people. He proclaimed that God's faithfulness was great and His mercy always new (Lamentations 3:22-23). Let's live with God's faithfulness always in mind. He is a good God, and always has the best interests of His people in mind. Learn to trust and rely on the goodness of God. In every trial, He will bring you through and will never leave you nor forsake you. Let's praise God for His great love and mercy, just as Jeremiah did!

Jeremiah's weeping came not from his weakness but from his strength, which was his relationship with God. May we have the same concern for our friends, family, and nation as he had.

CHAPTER 32: EZEKIEL - VISIONARY PROPHET (EZEKIEL 1-48)

About two years ago, I went for LASIK surgery on my eyes. I was amazed by the instant difference that the surgery provided! Whereas I used to only be able to see clearly with contacts or glasses, I now could see a clear image every time I opened my eyes. Suddenly, I could see with clarity, and I have never regretted having the operation done.

Ezekiel was an Old Testament prophet who saw clearly into the spirit. He prophesied with tremendous accuracy and authority, and his words still bring life and strength today. Ezekiel lived in a time when Judah was greatly backslidden and taken into captivity, about 600 years before the time of Christ. His words brought rebuke and comfort to the people. Ezekiel saw through the Spirit at least four different things that are relevant for us today.

1. Ezekiel saw the glory of God (Ezekiel 8-11). Ezekiel had several visions of the literal glory of God. He saw the glory of God leaving His people as a result of their sin, but then he saw the return of the glory when the people are restored. Ezekiel fell on his face before God's glory, and so we should stand in awe of how great God truly is. God's glory is a real entity that He wants to manifest in our churches and our lives. Let's ask God that He would give us a glimpse of how glorious He truly is.

2. Ezekiel saw the judgment and goodness of God (Ezekiel 1-7, 12-36). The book of Ezekiel is full of warnings and judgments against God's backslidden people and the wicked nations surrounding them. God will not tolerate the despising of His commands. However, Ezekiel also wrote many promises of restoration to the Israelites. Yes, God would judge them, but restoration would come if they turned back to Him. We always need to remember that God is a God of righteousness and if we live in disobedience we are subject to His wrath. We must not trifle with God. Even greater than His wrath, however, is His mercy, which He will show us when we cry out to Him in faith and repentance.

3. Ezekiel saw the army of God (Ezekiel 37). Ezekiel saw a vision of a valley full of dry bones. God prompted him to prophesy to these bones, and they began to rattle and come together. Ezekiel then commanded the bones to have muscle and skin, and finally God spoke through him that the bones must come to life! They became a powerful army for God. We may sometimes feel like we are as useless and dead as a dry bone, but God will always revive His faithful people. Let's not lie in the valley any longer, but allow God to raise us up to join His powerful, salvation - bringing last day army.

4. Ezekiel saw the dwelling of God (Ezekiel 40-48). The book of Ezekiel concludes with his vision of a future millennial temple in Jerusalem. This temple will be the dwelling place of God in the millennium and is full of His glory. The temple is a picture of our lives, as we are currently the dwelling places in which God desires to live. We don't only want to be visited by God, but we want to press in for His habitation - God inside of us at all times. There is nothing greater than to be His dwelling place, so let's seek the presence of God in our lives!

Ezekiel was a man of faith and vision. He easily could have given up on God and the people, as his nation was in captivity, but instead he allowed God to show him the wonderful plans He had for the nation. Let's be like Ezekiel and not get caught up in what our natural eyes see, but instead ask God to help us see things from His perspective.

CHAPTER 33: DANIEL - PURITY ON PURPOSE (DANIEL 1-12)

For a moment, imagine that you're thirsty. You've been outside, sweating in the hot sun. Maybe you've been playing soccer and haven't had a drink for an hour. Someone then comes up to you and offers you a nice, tall glass of water. You're so happy, but then you discover that the water is black and filthy. You turn away in disgust and ask what's wrong with the water. "Nothing's wrong!" the person replies. "This is 98% pure water. It's only 2% dirt, but 98% pure! Isn't that good enough?" I think you would probably turn away from that drink and wait for the next, 100% pure glass to come around!

Likewise, God desires complete purity in our lives. This doesn't mean that we never, ever make a mistake, but rather that we allow God to deal with every area of sin in our lives. We don't hold any sin back from His cleansing power. That is true purity, and a Bible character who exemplifies purity perhaps better than any other is Daniel. Daniel was a prophet, leader, and godly man. The book of Daniel covers over 70 years of his life, starting when he was about 16 years old. We will look at four areas of Daniel's life that stemmed from his purity before God.

1. Daniel was not stopped by difficult circumstances (Daniel 1:1-21). When Daniel was about 16 years old, he was taken from his home country of Judah to be a captive of the wicked Babylonian empire. He was taken from his family and all he had ever known, was given a new name, and had to learn a new language and a completely new culture. Babylon was the most wicked kingdom on earth, yet Daniel remained pure. How did he do it? Daniel "purposed in his heart" that he would not be defiled (Daniel 1:8). He was determined to find grace in the eyes of God and believed God could give him righteousness in any situation. You may find yourself in difficult circumstances at home or school, but you do not have to be a victim of those circumstances. Be a Daniel and determine to be a victor in every situation.

2. Daniel heard from God (Daniel 2:1-49, 4:1-37). Daniel had an extraordinary ability to interpret visions and dreams from God. There are many examples of this in the book of Daniel. One of the most outstanding examples took place when King Nebuchadnezzar had a dream that he could not remember. Daniel was able to tell Nebuchadnezzar what the dream was, and then accurately interpret what it meant. Daniel had astounding prophetic insight and predicted world events that were hundreds and even thousands of years away from occurring. Daniel's inspiration stemmed from his purity. God honored his walk of faith and told Daniel the secrets of His heart. God is still looking for friends He can share His heart with today.

3. Daniel did not fear man (Daniel 3:1-30, 5:1-31). Daniel's purity often forced him to make unpopular stands. His three friends Shadrach, Meshach, and Abednego also refused to give in to the ungodly demands of sinful men. God consistently delivered Daniel and his friends, and gave them great courage to do what was right in any situation. If we are going to be pure, there will be times when we have to do things that are greatly unpopular. Let's not fear man, but fear God who has called us to purity.

4. *Daniel stood out from those around him (Daniel 6:1-12:13).* Daniel's purity caused him to be so excellent in everything he did that he was promoted by king after king. The other leaders of the nation became very jealous of him and tricked one of the kings into signing an order banning anyone from praying to God. Daniel, of course, refused to obey this order, and continued praying three times a day. As a result, he was thrown alive into a den of hungry lions. Miraculously, God shut the mouth of the lions and Daniel was not touched! He was delivered from death because he trusted in God. Purity will make you outstanding as you stay humble before God and trust in Him.

Let's ask God to give us a pure heart as he gave unto Daniel. His purity was the basis for all of his outstanding accomplishments in life. It is the pure in heart that will see God (Matthew 5:8). Do you want to see Him? I know I do, so let's seek purity in our lives.

CHAPTER 34: ESTHER - COURAGE
(ESTHER 1-10)

When I was 9 years old, I remember going to a rally where the President of the United States, Ronald Reagan, was speaking. It was a thrill to see the President in real life. There he was, the leader of the country, speaking right in front of me! Now, when I saw President Reagan, it was in a crowded auditorium with many people around. But I still realized this was an important moment and I needed to be on my best behavior. Have you ever met a president, prime minister, or another important leader? How did you respond?

In this section we're going to read about Esther, a young lady who met the king of an entire empire. However, Esther not only met the king, she became his wife, the queen. God caused Esther to become queen at just the right moment, a moment where Esther would have the opportunity to save her people. And Esther showed tremendous courage in doing so. She risked her own life so that others could be saved, and in so doing is a tremendous model of courage for us. We can see four qualities of courage displayed in Esther's life.

1. *Courage enables us to be chosen (Esther 1:1-2:23).* King Ahasuerus, ruler of the Persian empire, decided to replace the rebellious Queen Vashti. Esther entered the king's house along with many other maidens to await her chance to meet the king. She bravely left behind her home and was willing to start a whole new life. When it came time for her to meet the king, she humbly listened to the advice of her elders and did not make any demands of her own. The king loved Esther and chose her to be his next queen. Her courage to leave her old life behind enabled her to be chosen for much greater things.

2. *Courage makes us willing to lay down our life (Esther 3:1-4:17).* King Ahasuerus' most trusted servant was a wicked man named Haman. Haman was angry that Esther's uncle, the godly Mordecai, would not bow before him and thus convinced Ahasuerus to sign an order to kill all the Jews in the kingdom (the king did not know Esther was a Jew). Mordecai went to Esther and asked her to go before the king and intercede on behalf of the Jews. Esther knew that no one, not even the queen, was allowed to go into the king's presence if he did not ask for them; the penalty for such an action was death. However, she decided to risk her life and go before him to plead for the salvation of the Jews. She considered the salvation of her people more important than her own life. We should likewise be willing to surrender everything to see the salvation of our generation.

3. *Courage causes us to make bold requests (Esther 5:1-7:10).* Esther did boldly go into the king's presence. She found favor in his sight and he extended his staff to her, saving her life. Two nights later, while the king and Haman were at a banquet Esther was hosting, she revealed to the king that she was a Jew and Haman was plotting to kill her and her people. The king was outraged and demanded that Haman be killed for his actions. Esther was not afraid to make bold requests to the king. Likewise, we should be willing to go before our King and ask Him for the salvation of souls. There is no need to be frightened, for He has provided us with His grace (Hebrews 4:16).

4. Courage brings deliverance to our people (Esther 8:1-10:3). After the king punished Haman, he declared that the Jews would be allowed to defend themselves against their enemies. The day when the Jews had been sentenced to be exterminated instead became a day of great victory over their enemies. Instead of being killed, Mordecai became the second most powerful man in the kingdom, and Esther continued to reign as queen.

Esther's courage saved the Jewish people from destruction. May we have the courage to spread the saving Gospel to our generation as well. The Gospel is the power of God and we need never be ashamed to proclaim it (Romans 1:16)!

CHAPTER 35: EZRA - STRENGTH
(EZRA 7-NEHEMIAH 12)

Some people say that Phil Pfister is the strongest man in the world. The 31-year-old American is 2 meters tall and weighs 156 kilos. He has done many incredible deeds, including lifting a platform on which *fifteen* children were standing! He has also pulled two 18-wheeler semi-trucks over a distance of 100 feet *at the same time*. Phil is definitely not someone I would want to face in an arm-wrestling match!

As impressive as those things are, in this section we will be looking at a much stronger man - Ezra the priest. Ezra's strength was displayed not through physical exploits but through the courageous way in which he served God's people. Servanthood is a great strength. He ministered in a time of restoration, when the Jews were being returned to their land and brought back into God's purposes (a little more than 400 years before the time of Christ). There are four different ways we will consider in which Ezra's strength was shown.

1. Ezra's strength was shown as a teacher of God's Law (Ezra 7:1-10). Ezra was a scribe who studied and loved the ways of God. He burned with a passion for God's Word and explained God's ways to the people. Our lives should always be built on the foundation of God's Word. It contains all true life and spiritual power.

2. Ezra's strength was shown in building up God's temple (Ezra 7:11-8:36). Ezra obtained permission from the king to lead a large group of Jews back to Jerusalem. One of their tasks was to beautify and improve the temple, which had been rebuilt about 80 years previously. Ezra had a passion for the dwelling place of God and sacrificed in order to strengthen it. He lived a life of service to God and His people and brought great benefit through this service. Ask God how you can have a part in building up your local church and ministries as Ezra did.

3. Ezra's strength was shown in returning the people to righteousness (Ezra 9:1-10:44). When Ezra arrived in Jerusalem, he found that many of the people there had backslidden and turned away from God. He took authority in these situations and led the people into repentance and reformation. Ezra was not afraid to be unpopular but he took a stand for righteousness. He is a powerful example for us to follow, as we live in an age when most people don't want to hear that what they are doing is wrong. Let's be like Ezra and never shy away from spreading God's righteous message to our backslidden generation.

4. Ezra's strength was shown by assisting in the last revival in the Old Testament (Nehemiah 1:1-12:31). After Ezra had gone to Jerusalem, Nehemiah was the next great leader who followed him. Ezra assisted Nehemiah in bringing about another revival, which was the last return to God recorded in the Old Testament Scriptures. Ezra was willing to help Nehemiah fulfill God's call on his life. We should also be willing and eager to help others who are carrying God's message. We are a part of the Kingdom of God and it takes partnership with others to bring about His greater purposes.

Ezra's strength of character helped change a nation and prepare the world for the coming of Jesus. Strength of character is more valuable than strength of body, and is something that is available to each and every believer through Christ. Let's have the strength of Ezra and make an impact in our world!

CHAPTER 36: NEHEMIAH - GOD'S BUILDER (NEHEMIAH 1-13)

One of my favorite toys when I was young boy was a set of soft, large building blocks. The only problem was that I was never very good at building things with my hands! Most of the time I would only create pulpits so I could pretend to preach, or use the blocks as a bat and bases so I could play balloon baseball! Of course, my friends who were better at building could form houses, shelters, and a host of other things.

Nehemiah was an expert builder. He lived about 400 years before the time of Christ and led the Jews to rebuild the walls of Jerusalem. Amazingly, his strong leadership enabled them to build the walls of the city in just fifty-two days despite strong opposition. Through Nehemiah's life, we can learn at least four lessons about building for God.

1. Nehemiah built through prayer (Nehemiah 1:1-11). Throughout his life, Nehemiah was a man of prayer. His prayers are recorded over and over; he would pray in every situation. He was never shy about asking for God's help. He had a heart of compassion for his people, the Jews, and asked for God's aid in their time of need. If we are going to be used to build God's Kingdom in our generation, we also need to ask largely of God. Our prayers should be bold, persistent, and faith-filled.

2. Nehemiah built by being willing to give up his position (Nehemiah 2:1-3:32). Nehemiah had a comfortable position in the Persian empire as cupbearer to the king. He lived in the king's palace and was a trusted friend to the most powerful man on earth. However, he asked the king if he could leave this job to go and build the walls of Jerusalem. The king granted his request, and Nehemiah left his life of privilege and comfort behind to go and build something for God. We need to be willing to give up our comforts as well if God is going to use us to build great things. Some of you may have to leave your nation; some your riches; all of us have to leave our reputation. Be willing to give up your lifestyle for God's kingdom.

3. Nehemiah built in the face of opposition (Nehemiah 4:1-6:19). When the enemies of the Jews heard that they were going to rebuild the walls, they threatened them and planned to bring their armies against the city. Nehemiah rallied the people to stand watch and continue building the walls. His courage in the face of danger inspired the people and led them to complete their task; moreover, God protected His people and no harm came to the Jews. There will always be enemy opposition when we are doing a work for God, but stand strong and God will fight your battle. Never give in to the enemy.

4. Nehemiah built in righteousness (Nehemiah 7:1-13:31). Nehemiah brought the last great revival recorded in the Old Testament. He dealt with sin severely and punished the backslidden Jews in order to turn them back to God. Nehemiah was serious with sin and God honored his commitment for righteousness. Let's make sure that righteousness is at the foundation of every work we do for God. It's not enough only to do works for God, but we must have His character worked inside of us. Then we can build in a way that's truly pleasing to Him!

God has called each one of us to build for him, in our personal lives and ministries. Nehemiah is a model of a godly builder that we should all emulate.

CHAPTER 37: MARY AND JOSEPH - FAVOR (MATTHEW 1, LUKE 1-2)

I remember the excitement my wife and I experienced when we found out we were going to have our first child. It was such great news - a new life was going to come into the world and into our family! At the same time, there was also a sense of nervousness and trepidation; we were going to be responsible for this new life at all times. Were we really ready to be parents?

Now imagine for a moment how Mary and Joseph must have felt when they found out that not only were they going to have a son, but the one and only Son of God. It was a mind-blowing honor to be chosen as the natural parents of Jesus Christ. We are told that Mary was highly blessed by God, for she had found favor in His eyes. God's favor is His blessings and grace being freely given to us. Favor is not something we can earn, but something that God gives to us even though we do not deserve it. Yet there are certain characteristics we should have if we desire the favor of God, and we can learn four of them from the lives of Mary and Joseph.

1. Mary and Joseph lived lives of purity (Luke 1:1-37). Mary and Joseph both kept themselves sexually pure in their engagement. When Mary was told she would be giving birth to Jesus, she was amazed as she was still a virgin. However, she accepted this responsibility with humble submission. They were obedient to the call of God. Their lives of purity attracted God's favor, and it is the same for us today. In the midst of an immoral age, we can ask God to give us grace to remain pure before Him.

2. Mary and Joseph were worshippers (Luke 1:38-80). Mary's famous exclamation of praise to God is seen when she meets her cousin Elizabeth, mother of John the Baptist. We see that Mary and Joseph rejoiced in God at all times and were in awe of His greatness. We also know that they visited the temple often, faithfully worshipping God. Worship is essential in our lives as well, not just when singing in worship during services but also in our own time with God. We must adore Him for all that He is.

3. Mary and Joseph valued the approval of God over that of man (Matthew 1:1-25). When Joseph first heard that Mary was pregnant, he thought she must have committed immorality with another man and was going to end the engagement. However, an angel told him that the child was from God, so Joseph quickly supported Mary. Mary and Joseph were both willing to bear this shame in order to bring God's purposes to pass. If we truly want God's favor, we need to be more concerned with His opinion than that of man.

4. Mary and Joseph were focused on heavenly and not earthly blessing (Luke 2:1-52). Mary and Joseph knew the favor of God was more about spiritual blessing than earthly. When Christ was born, they were not even able to get a room in an inn. They even had limited resources to offer when they dedicated Christ, offering a turtledove (which was the offering given by the poorest class of people). Yet they never complained, as they knew the favor of God was upon them and He was blessing them greatly. When we seek God's favor, let's make sure it is with an eye towards His spiritual blessings rather than earthly riches. God's favor will make us rich spiritually, and that is the blessing we should seek!

Let's pray for God's favor to be on our lives. He desires to show it to His children, and as we live in a way that is conducive to receiving His blessings, He will pour them out on us.

CHAPTER 38: SIMEON - GOD'S PROMISES (LUKE 2:25-35)

One of the first memories I have occurred when I was about five years old. I specifically remember one day when my Mom told me we would be going out later to Baskin Robbins for ice cream. I was so excited! I remember actually rolling on the ground and waiting for that beautiful ice cream cone. And then later that night, the promise was fulfilled; I got my ice cream cone and have not stopped eating ice cream since!

Simeon is a Biblical character who also received a promise and saw it come to pass. Of course, Simeon's promise was of a much greater quality and came from God Himself! God promised him that he would not die until he had seen Christ, the Messiah in the flesh. God desires to give each of us wonderful promises as well. Although Simeon's life story is only mentioned in a few short verses, we can learn several lessons about how to obtain God's promises by studying it, four of which we will look at here.

1. *Simeon realized God had to give the promise (Luke 2:25-26).* The Holy Spirit revealed to Simeon that he would not die until he had seen the coming of Jesus. Simeon did not make up the promise on his own, but it came directly from God. Likewise, a true godly promise is not something we create from our desires, but rather a reality from God. Spend time asking God what He wants to do in your life, and let His desires become your own.

2. *Simeon patiently waited for the promise (Luke 2:27).* Simeon was an elderly man when Jesus was born. However, he never gave up believing that Israel's Savior would come. It was the Holy Spirit that led him to the temple on the day he saw the baby Jesus; his sensitivity to God allowed him to hear and receive. He actively sought God while waiting for the promise and walked in the Spirit. He didn't allow himself to get caught up in earthly affairs but kept his focus on God. It is through faith and patience that we obtain God's promises (Hebrews 6:12). Never grow weary of waiting but believe God until His word comes to pass.

3. *Simeon received the fulfillment of the promise (Luke 2:28).* After a long period of waiting in faith, the day came when Simeon saw the Messiah. It was on the eighth day of Jesus' life, when His parents brought Him to the temple to be dedicated to God. Simeon saw the baby Jesus and held Him in his arms, blessing God. It is not enough for us to just hear a promise of God, but like Simeon we must be faithful until we receive the fulfillment. God's promises are all true, so press in until you receive all that He has spoken.

4. *Simeon rejoiced in the promise (Luke 2:29-35).* Simeon rejoiced and blessed God as he held the baby Jesus. It was a truly amazing moment for the man Simeon, as mortality held immortality. The hands that had formed mountains were now the hands of the tiny baby gripping his finger; the One who had always existed was now cradled in his arms. Simeon's heart was full of joy and thanksgiving to God. Let's be faithful to always praise God and rejoice in His goodness when His promises to us are fulfilled. Our proper response will invite God to give us more of His wonderful promises.

God is a good God and desires to give wonderful promises to His children. Regardless of whether we are young or old, let's follow Simeon's example and allow ourselves to be receivers of God's promise. Praise God for His goodness to us at all times!

CHAPTER 39: JOHN THE BAPTIST - MESSENGER (MATTHEW 3:1-17, 11:1-19)

Some of you may be too young to have experienced this, but I remember a few years back when AOL and Windows Instant Messenger first became widespread. It seemed amazing at the time; it was so easy to have real time conversations over the Internet! Email had come a few years before, but that didn't give you the immediacy of the instant message. It was great to be able to spread information in such a simple, quick way.

Messengers have always been important, whether they were the runners of ancient times, the postman of last century, or the computers of today. The most important messenger the world has ever seen, however, was a man named John the Baptist. He was born only a few months before Christ and had a specific mission from God to prepare the way for the Messiah. He labored faithfully to point people to Jesus. We are also called to be messengers for God, and can learn four things about being a faithful, fiery messenger from John the Baptist's life.

1. The messenger lives in complete obedience to God (Matthew 3:1-4). John the Baptist was called to minister from the desert, and that's what he did. He lived a lifestyle of radical devotion, giving up all earthly comforts in order to obey the call of God. He dressed in a camel's coat, and he ate grasshoppers and wild honey. God is not going to call most of us to go live in the wilderness and eat insects, but let's be willing to give up every material thing that he asks us to in order to fulfill His will. Obedience is always better than earthly comfort and possessions, and we can only faithfully deliver God's message while living in this obedience.

2. The messenger calls people to radical repentance (Matthew 3:5-10). John the Baptist did not hold back his words when calling the people to repentance. He confronted the sins of the nation with incredible boldness. He began water-baptizing people, as a sign that their sins were being washed away and they could now walk in righteousness. A faithful messenger must never compromise with sin but rather bravely proclaim God's righteousness and holy standard. We cannot try to be friends of the world but should instead be radical in our commitment to righteousness.

3. The messenger points attention to Christ and the Holy Spirit (Matthew 3:11-17). Because of his great power and ministry, people began wondering if John was the Messiah. He faithfully proclaimed that he was not, but that Christ was soon to be revealed. When Jesus came to be baptized by him, he let the people know that this was the Lamb of God. John also proclaimed that Jesus would baptize in the Holy Spirit and fire, a greater baptism than that of water. As messengers today, we must always seek to deflect all attention from ourselves and point it to Jesus. Our ministry is not in our power but the power of the Holy Spirit.

4. The messenger receives praise from God (Matthew 11:1-19). John the Baptist was eventually imprisoned and beheaded by wicked king Herod. When the people came to Jesus and asked Him about John, Jesus declared that he was the greatest man ever born of a woman. It was a tremendous commendation from God Himself. John the Baptist's message did not gain him love from the world but praise from God. Let's always aim for heaven's approval rather than this world's. Man's praise is temporary, but God's is eternal!

There was only one John the Baptist, but God is looking for many other "messengers" today who will boldly proclaim that Christ has come and is coming once again. Let's be true heralds for Him.

CHAPTER 40: PETER (PART 1) - INSTABILITY (MATTHEW-JOHN)

Several years ago when I was doing mission work in India one of my fellow missionaries had a scooter he used to get around. He asked me if I wanted to learn how to use it and I agreed. We went to a remote road and I got behind the handlebars for the first time. Nervous, I accelerated and the scooter began to go forward. I had only traveled a few meters when I felt the scooter tipping. I tried to adjust but ended up falling down and almost running the scooter down to the rice fields several meters below! I learned that riding a scooter is not like riding a bicycle and my instability cost me a lot of embarrassment and almost cost me a lot of pain!

Peter is one of the great heroes of the New Testament and was a leader among the twelve apostles. Yet, the first part of his life and ministry was marked by great instability. This inconsistency plagued him and he could not be counted on in times of need. He would have a great triumph and then follow it with a great failure. Of course, God changed Peter in time. We want to learn to be reliable in our walk with God, and we will look at four lessons on instability we can learn from the early life of Peter.

1. Peter's instability did not keep him from being called by Christ (Mark 1:16-17,3:16). Though Peter was an unstable man, Jesus still called him to be his disciple. Peter was fishing with his brother Andrew when Jesus asked them to follow Him. To his great credit, Peter instantly obeyed and left his nets behind. Later, Jesus gave him the name Peter (he previously was called Simon), which means, "rock." Christ saw that Peter would become a stable rock even though he was then a weak believer. Be encouraged that we do not have to be perfect for God to call us; we can be transformed if we will just be obedient to yield to His call.

2. Peter's instability was displayed in his impetuous speech (Mark 8:31-33,9:1-10). Peter had a tendency of always saying the wrong thing at the wrong time. Once he argued vehemently with Christ that He did not need to be crucified. Jesus then rebuked Peter for letting Satan speak through him! On the Mount of Transfiguration, Peter suggested building tabernacles for the glorified Christ, Moses, and Elijah because the situation was so amazing and he did not know what else to say. Peter always had a need to say something. Allow God to teach you to be patient in your speech and not to unwisely speak when you don't have anything to say, particularly when you are in God's presence.

3. Peter's instability conflicted with his great faith (Matthew 14:24-32). Though Peter was unstable, he also had great faith. His great faith can be seen when he stepped out of the boat and walked with Jesus *on the water.* This was an amazing act of faith. However, his instability was seen as he grew afraid and began looking at the waves around him; then he sank. Let's be inspired by the faith of Peter but also be warned that to continue in the miraculous, we must keep our eyes fixed on Jesus.

4. Peter's instability led to his greatest failure (Mark 14:50-72). Jesus warned His disciples that they would desert Him when He was arrested, but Peter argued that He would never turn away from God. However, when the dark moment arrived, Peter denied even knowing Jesus three times. It was a crushing, devastating failure.

Peter was unstable because he relied on his own power and not the grace of God. Let's learn to rely on God's strength and not our own. Peter learned the lesson and became a great example and a rock in God's Kingdom, as we will see in the next chapter.

CHAPTER 41: PETER (PART 2) - STABLE AS A ROCK (JOHN 21-ACTS, 1 PETER-2 PETER)

A few years ago, when I was in India, a large group of us went swimming in a river quite far away. We had a great time as this was an unusual treat for us all. One thing I remember about the river is the large rocks that were scattered throughout. These rocks made great places to lie on and rest after expending energy in the water. They were also a place of safety from the jagged stones and slippery terrain below.

There are few things more stable than a large rock. God wants us have to have spiritual stability, where we can be relied upon in the middle of any environment. Peter was an extraordinary apostle of Christ whose name (which was given by Jesus) comes from the Greek word "petras", meaning "rock." Although he was inconsistent early in his life and ministry, he became a source of stability and the leader of the Early Church after the Ascension of Christ. We can learn four lessons about stability from his life.

1. Peter's stability came through supernatural restoration from Christ (John 21:1-25). The greatest failure of Peter's life came during the trial and crucifixion of Jesus, where he denied being a follower of Christ three times. After this tragic event, Peter surely thought God would not give him another chance to follow Him. However, Jesus appeared to the disciples several times after His resurrection. On one of these occasions, He gave Peter a special message and a specific charge to take care of His people. Jesus confirmed His love to Peter and let him know he would have another chance. This experience changed Peter forever. He would never again waver in his devotion to Christ. We all need a revelation of God's love and forgiveness in order to give us the confidence to have a stable relationship with Him.

2. Peter's stability enabled him to lead the greatest revival the Church has ever seen (Acts 1:1-9:43). Peter emerged as the leader of the apostles after they were all filled with the Holy Spirit on the Day of Pentecost. That very day he preached a bold message and three thousand people were saved. Many thousands more were saved, healed, and delivered through his ministry as the revival continued. Peter was able to lead the revival because his faith in Christ and relationship with Him was secure. God cannot entrust revival to moody, up-and-down, Christians. Let's have stability so He can do great works through our lives.

3. Peter's stability was the basis from which he reached out to the Gentiles (Acts 10:1-12:25). For many years, the early Christians only evangelized to Jews. Peter was the first to reach out to the despised Gentiles and bring them the message of salvation. This was a radical thing for a Jew to do, but it was exactly what God wanted to happen. Peter could do radical things because his foundation was stable. God calls us to live outside of the box of tradition and archaic religion, but we can only do that when we ourselves are stable in our faith.

4. Peter's stability was passed down to others (1 Peter 1:1-2 Peter 3:18). Peter was a father to many in the faith and towards the end of his life wrote the epistles of 1st and 2nd Peter. One theme of these great letters is being established and settled in the faith. Peter was able to minister on these themes because of the amazing transformation God had brought in his own life. Our stability can be transmitted to those younger in the faith. Let's be an inspiring example that other believers can follow.

The time for up and down, yo-yo Christianity is over. God doesn't want our relationship with Him to be one of emotional swings but of faith and confidence. Peter gives us great hope; if we've been inconsistent in the past, God can completely change us! Stability is a mark of spiritual maturity. Let's ask God to work this great quality in our lives.

CHAPTER 42: WOMAN CAUGHT IN THE ACT OF ADULTERY-GOD'S FORGIVENESS (JOHN 8:1-11)

Have you ever been caught doing something that you knew you were not supposed to do? Now, hopefully this doesn't happen to you every day, and hopefully you have reached a point where you no longer do things that you know are wrong. But at some point in our lives, I think all of us have had this happen, whether we were caught speeding by the police, cheating by our teacher, or taking an extra cookie by our mother! It's a scary thing to be caught in the act.

The book of John tells the story of a woman caught in the act of adultery. We do not know her actual name, but we do know that her life was changed by God. This story is one of the most shining examples of God's mercy and forgiveness in all of Scripture, and can serve as an inspiration for all of us. We can learn four lessons about God's forgiveness from the experience of this woman.

1. God's forgiveness can cover the worst of sins (John 8:1-5). The woman in this story had been caught in the very act of committing adultery. Adultery, of course, is forbidden by the Ten Commandments and is a very serious offense against God. She was being unfaithful and sinning in such a shameful way that she could be caught in public by the Pharisees. However, God still forgave her of this sin. This forgiveness gives us hope that it does not matter what mistakes we have made in the past; God will forgive all who come by faith and ask Him for forgiveness.

2. God's forgiveness is not understood by the proud (John 8:6-8). The Pharisees who caught this woman committing her sin knew that God's Law declared that the punishment for adultery was murder. They were jealous of Jesus and wanted to trap Him, so they brought the woman before Him. They reasoned Jesus would either have to put her to death, thus bypassing mercy, or say she should live, thus disobeying the Law. Jesus, however, seemed to ignore the Pharisees question. He simply wrote on the ground and then said that whoever had no sin could cast the first stone. The Pharisees and other leaders could never understand the forgiveness of God because of their pride. If we want to receive forgiveness for our sins, we must come to God in humility.

3. God's forgiveness is based in His righteousness (John 8:9-10). After Jesus made the statement showing the leaders their own sinfulness, everyone left except Him and the woman. The reason Jesus could stay is because He was the only One who truly was sinless. He was perfectly righteous. The basis from which God forgives our sinfulness is His righteousness. Only a perfectly righteous God can atone for and forgive sins. Thank God for His righteousness and believe Him to share it with you on a daily basis.

4. God's forgiveness is given not just to pardon us but to change us (John 8:11). When Jesus was left alone with the woman, He offered her forgiveness, telling her that He would not condemn her. However, He also gave her this charge, "Now go, and sin no more." Jesus didn't only forgive the woman; He also gave her the command to be righteous and the hope of change. God forgives us in order to make us holy and transform us. Forgiveness is not just focused on the past but also on changing our future. Thank God that by His grace we can go forward and sin no more!

God's forgiveness is truly remarkable. As sinners, we deserve nothing but judgment and death, but God chooses to shower His mercy and forgiveness upon us instead. He forgives us in order to change us and transform us to be more like Him. Let's praise Him for His forgiving, transforming power.

CHAPTER 43: RICH YOUNG RULER - COVETOUSNESS (MARK 10:17-27)

Have you ever started eating a snack and been unable to stop? I think it's happened to all of us. You just meant to have one potato chip, peanut, or chocolate; next thing you know you're eating and eating and you're not able to stop. The more you have, the more you want!

This desire for more is a basic problem to mankind, especially as it applies to matters more important than snacks. Covetousness is a terrible sin that can be clearly seen in the life of a man who is commonly called "The Rich Young Ruler". This man met Jesus and was given the opportunity to follow Him and be a disciple, but tragically chose his riches over Christ. He desired a rich lifestyle instead of serving God. We can learn at least four lessons about the terrible dangers of covetousness from his life.

1. The young man's covetousness did not satisfy his desires (Mark 10:17). Despite his riches and position of authority, the young man knew that there was something more to life. He ran to Christ and knelt before Him, hoping that Christ could fulfill the longing in his heart. He had amassed great riches but derived no satisfaction from them. This shows us that earthly possessions and achievements are empty. Do not seek after the things of this world but rather seek the One who created you to know Him.

2. The young man's covetousness was disguised by his pride (Mark 10:18-20). Jesus told the young man to obey the commandments if he wanted eternal life. The ruler responded by saying that he had obeyed all from his childhood. He may have been a good man on the outside, but he was proud to think he had kept all of God's laws, as all have sinned. His pride kept him from noticing his greedy desire for things, and it can be the same for us. Let us ask God for humility and contentment so that we do not fall into this trap.

3. The young man's covetousness was confronted by Christ (Mark 10:21). There was something about this rich young ruler that caused Jesus to especially love him. Jesus gave him the invitation to sell all he had and be a disciple, following Christ. Jesus wanted the young man to be His follower, but knew that first the covetousness needed to be taken from the young man's life. We are also called to be disciples, and in the process God will have to confront issues in our life (including greed and covetousness). Thank God when He confronts the sin in your life, and let's be faithful to yield to Him and repent.

4. The young man's covetousness ultimately ruined his life (Mark 10:22-27). When the young man heard this command, he turned away in sorrow. He chose his possessions over the chance to follow Jesus. He wasn't satisfied in following God but wanted the things of this world. The rest of his life (and even into eternity) he surely lived in regret, knowing that he had missed his chance and the call of God on his life. Covetousness will also ruin us, if we do not let God remove it from our lives.

The desire to be rich leads men to destruction. The Gospel is always focused on heavenly riches, and not the things of this world. When we have Christ, we have all we ever need, in heaven or on earth! Let's ask God to remove all covetousness from our lives and even from our faith.

CHAPTER 44: BARTIMEAUS - DESPERATION (MARK 10:46-52)

Some of my best memories from high school come from my experiences on the school basketball team. I had a great time, though I never had the most accurate shooting, best ball handling, fastest feet, or biggest frame (especially in my first couple of years on the team). One thing I always did have, however, was desperation for the basketball. I would do anything to get a rebound or grab a loose ball, no matter how many bruises or floor burns it gave me! I remember once I jumped into a crowd of cheerleaders in order to throw a ball over my head back onto the court. My teammate picked up the ball and hit a three pointer, and no cheerleaders were harmed in the making of the play. My desperation served me well!

Desperation is also an important quality in our spiritual lives. God wants us to be desperate for His Spirit and power and not be content with mediocre living. Bartimaeus is a shining example of desperation. He was a blind beggar who sat by the road each day in a sad existence, but ended up being healed by Christ . If we want revival and the supernatural in our lives, we need humility to realize our need for God. There are four lessons we can learn about desperation from Bartimaeus' life.

1. Bartimaeus' desperation caused him to call out to Christ (Mark 10:46-47). Bartimaeus was sitting by the highway begging, much as he probably did each day. When he heard that Jesus was passing by this road, however, he knew that it was not just another day. He began to cry out for Jesus to have mercy on him. He lifted his voice and cried for God's favor. This fact is important for us to note; desperation is never quiet. Let's cry out in prayer with desperation for God to move in our generation. Desperation will always cause us to lift our voice.

2. Bartimaeus' desperation led to the crowd being disturbed (Mark 10:48). As he continued to cry out for Jesus above the noise of the crowd, Bartimaeus grew louder and louder. Those around him began to get annoyed and told him to be quiet, but this caused him to shout all the louder. Bartimaeus would not let the opinions of others keep him from receiving his miracle. Always remember, you are serving God and not man. Pray and worship with a focus on what will please God; do not be stopped by the disapproving stares of proud man.

3. Bartimaeus' desperation attracted Christ (Mark 10:49-50). When Jesus heard Bartimaeus, He stopped walking and stood still. He then commanded Bartimaeus to come stand before Him. There were most likely many beggars with problems along that same road, but the Bible only records Jesus stopping for Bartimaeus. The desperation in his heart attracted the compassion of Christ. Jesus always shows up strong for those whose hearts are wholly after Him. Your desperation will draw you out of the crowd and attract the touch of God.

4. Bartimaeus' desperation brought his miracle (Mark 10:51-52). When Bartimaeus stood before Jesus, He asked Jesus to give Him sight. Jesus healed him because of Bartimaeus' great faith. The desperation in his heart led to the impossible; a blind man could now see. Preachers commonly refer to him as "Blind Bartimaeus", but we should really call him "Seeing Bartimaeus" as Christ changed him forever! The first step in receiving a miracle is thus desperation.

If we are satisfied in our current condition we will always remain this way, but if we cry out in faith and humility for a new touch from God He will answer. Desperation is not something we can work up on our own, but must come from a genuine realization of our brokenness. Let's ask God to give us a new understanding of how badly we need Him.

CHAPTER 45: MARY AND MARTHA - ADORATION (LUKE 10, JOHN 11-12)

Imagine that your long-lost friend came for a visit. You were so excited that you would finally get a chance to catch up on old times! However, the entire time he was visiting your house, all he did was clean your room, wash your dishes, and iron your clothes. When he finishes these chores, the time has come when he has to go. He would have accomplished a lot, but you would be very sad that you had not gotten a chance to just spend time together!

Mary and Martha were two sisters who were friends of Jesus during His earthly ministry. They were both followers of Christ who believed in Him, but Mary had a deep adoration for God, while Martha was often busy doing things for Him. Mary realized spending time getting to know Christ was the ultimate thing, and she is most known for her adoration (or fervent and devoted love) of Jesus. We can learn at least four lessons about adoration by studying the lives of these two sisters.

1. Adoration is better than busy service (Luke 10:38-42). The first account of Mary and Martha takes place when Martha invited Jesus to her home for dinner. Martha was very busy serving the guests, while Mary was sitting at Jesus' feet. Martha became upset that her sister was not helping her and complained about it to Jesus. Jesus, however, pointed out that Mary had chosen the better part, sitting in His presence. Martha's service was good; Mary's adoration was better. It is good and necessary to serve God and do works for Him, but they must never be the priority in our lives. Rather, our worship and time spent alone with Him is always most important.

2. Adoration enables us to wait on God (John 11:1-29). Mary and Martha had a brother named Lazarus who died. Four days after his death, Jesus came to the funeral. Martha rushed up to Christ and bemoaned that He had not been there earlier to heal Lazarus. Mary, however, waited for Jesus to call for her before approaching. Mary and Martha both had faith that Jesus could heal, but Mary's heart of adoration gave her patience to wait on God's timing. When we adore Him as Lord, we will not rush Him but will be willing to wait for His time.

3. Adoration moves the heart of God in compassion (John 11:30-57). When Jesus saw the sadness of Mary and Martha over the death of Lazarus, He Himself wept. He had great compassion on the two sisters. Their adoration brought them close to God's heart and moved Him to raise Lazarus from the dead in an extraordinary miracle. Miracles flow out of a life of intimacy with God.

4. Adoration is extravagant (John 12:1-8). Shortly after Jesus raised Lazarus from the dead, the family once again had a dinner with Jesus as guest. Mary anointed the feet of Jesus with a pound of spikenard, which was incredibly costly. She worshipped Him by pouring the sweet spice upon Him. Some of the disciples were angry that the money was not given to the poor instead, but Jesus pointed out that she was doing it as an act of worship that would never be forgotten. Do not hold back in your worship and adoration of God, but give Him all of your strength, abilities, and talents.

God deserves all our worship forever, so we can never give Him more than He deserves. He is truly great, and is looking for those who will worship in spirit and in truth (John 4:23,24). Adore Him!

CHAPTER 46: MARY MAGDALENE - PASSION (MARK 16, JOHN 19-20)

My favorite American football team is the Detroit Lions. They have never won a championship in my lifetime. In fact, they have never won or *even played in* the Super Bowl in its 42 years of existence! Even more, they have actually been the single worst team in football during this decade, and continually fall short of the high hopes I set for them each year. So why do I keep cheering for them? Because they are my team, and I have a passion to see them win!

Mary Magdalene was a follower of Jesus who had a far greater passion. She followed Christ with an indistinguishable desire. Even at the darkest moments of the Gospel story, she stayed faithful to Him. Although she is only mentioned in a few short verses of the Bible, she is remembered throughout the world for her passion for Christ, and we will look at four lessons about passion from her life.

1. *Mary Magdalene's passion had its source in her miraculous deliverance (Mark 16:9).* Before she met Christ, Mary Magdalene was possessed by seven demons. Jesus delivered Mary from this demonic oppression and gave her true freedom. For the rest of her life, Mary knew that Christ had done a tremendous miracle for her and had great love and passion for Him. May we never forget the miracles God has done in our lives (starting with the miracle of salvation) so that our passion always burns bright for Him. Those who realize they have been forgiven much will love much.

2. *Mary Magdalene's passion caused her to stick with Christ through the darkest times (John 19:25-20:13).* Although all of the 12 apostles deserted Christ during His crucifixion, Mary Magdalene and a few other women remained at His side. Her love for Christ compelled her to stay with Him, even though she was risking her life by supporting a condemned man. After His crucifixion, she faithfully went to His tomb to pay respect to Him. Passion for God will empower us to keep serving Him even through dark and difficult times. Trials will come, but passion keeps us faithful!

3. *Mary Magdalene's passion was rewarded by having the first encounter with the resurrected Christ (John 20:17-17).* When visiting Jesus' tomb, Mary Magdalene was distraught that it was empty, thinking His body had been stolen. She saw a man and thought he was the gardener. She begged the man to tell her where Jesus' body had been laid. The man looked at her, and as He called her "Mary," she instantly knew that this was actually Jesus talking to her. She was the first person to see the resurrected Christ. It was a tremendous privilege she had. Passion brings us revelation! God shows Himself to the passionate.

4. *Mary Magdalene's passion led her to tell others about the resurrection (John 20:18).* After Mary had seen Jesus she ran back to the disciples to tell them that she had seen Christ and He was raised from the dead. Her passion made her the first evangelist of the Risen Lord. Passionate people are never quiet about their passion! Let's ask God to give us passion for Him so that we will be faithful to spread our faith to this lost and dying world.

We have all been forgiven and delivered by the Lord in miraculous ways. Mary Magdalene's life was forever changed by her deliverance, and she never, ever forgot what Christ had done for her. May we also have the passion of Mary Magdalene and have that same desire for the Lord!

CHAPTER 47: PAUL (PART 1) - GLORIOUS CONVERSION (ACTS 8-11)

Have you ever changed your mind? Maybe you had a strong opinion about something when you were younger but think in an entirely different manner today. I remember I used to like eating peas when I was a young boy. Now it's my least favorite vegetable and I don't want to see them anywhere near my plate! You can say I have been converted in my opinion of peas.

The Apostle Paul had the most glorious conversion recorded in the Bible. In a moment's time, he was changed from being a Christ-hater to a Christ-follower. A true conversion is a change in lifestyle, thinking, and vision; a change that takes place in our body, soul, and spirit. Outside of Christ, Paul is the greatest and most dominant figure of the New Testament. His life is so important that we will spend the next three chapters examining it, starting by learning four things about glorious conversions.

1. A glorious conversion can occur for the worst of sinners (Acts 8:1-9:2). Before his conversion, Paul (then known as Saul) was a leader of the Pharisees who went from town to town, violently searching out Christians to imprison and murder them. He was present at the murder of the Church's first martyr, Stephen. Paul was self-righteous, angry, and full of hatred toward Christ, yet Jesus reached out to Him, bringing salvation and conversion. Thus, we must never think it is impossible for God to save anyone. No matter how bad of a background you or someone you know has, God will save any who will turn to Him in faith and repentance.

2. A glorious conversion comes through an encounter with Christ (Acts 9:2-9). Paul was on his way to Damascus to persecute more Christians when he was knocked to the ground by a bright light. Jesus then spoke to him, asking why he was persecuting Christ. Paul instantly repented and asked Jesus what he should do. His conversion was glorious because he met Christ. If we wish to see true conversion in the life of others, we must always point them to Christ and pray that God will reveal Himself to the convert. It's not enough to just have people come to an altar call or repeat a prayer; they must meet Jesus for their lives to be truly changed.

3. A glorious conversion needs instruction from others (Acts 9:10-19). Around the same time as Paul was being converted, God appeared to a disciple named Ananias and told him that he was to meet Saul and pray for his sight to return (which he had lost when he saw the light). God also instructed Paul to go into Damascus and meet others who would tell him what to do. Even though Paul met Christ Himself, he still needed instruction from others in how to continue in the Christian walk. True conversion begins with an encounter with God, but God chooses to follow that with instruction from people. A newborn baby cannot feed himself but must be fed; so we must give instruction and guidance to new converts.

4. A glorious conversion is instant but takes time to be fully completed (Acts 9:20-11:24). After his conversion, Paul went straight to preach Christ in the synagogues. His passion was admirable, but he was not yet ready to be the awesome leader God had called him to be. He ended up spending the next twelve years in relative obscurity. When you are converted your heart will change immediately, but it will take time for God to build His character inside of you. Paul allowed God to complete the work in his life and the results were glorious.

Paul was completely changed through his meeting with Jesus. Conversion to Christ is always glorious. Let's take this message to the streets and bring true conversions into God's Kingdom.

CHAPTER 48: PAUL (PART 2) - MISSIONARY (ACTS 13-20)

I remember my first journey into long-term missionary work. I was 22 years old when I moved to India to work with Zion Ministries, and everything in that land was different. The sights, the smells, the way people drove, the animals roaming the streets; it was all so exotic! I loved the experience and the six months I stayed there and have spent most of my time since then as a full-time missionary. And one man in Scripture that I (and countless other missionaries!) have learned much from and try to emulate is the Apostle Paul.

The Apostle Paul went on three missionary journeys (each lasting several years) that are recorded in the book of Acts. He spread the message of Christ throughout the Roman Empire and had a singular passion to make God known. The man who once attempted to suppress Christianity became its greatest propagator. There are numerous lessons to learn from his missionary techniques, four of which we will examine.

1. The missionary must go to new places (Acts 13:1-14:28). Paul was together with other leaders of the Antioch church when the Holy Spirit spoke that Paul and Barnabas were to be sent out. On this journey they traveled wide, going to many places where Christ had never been preached. Paul stepped out of his comfort zone and left the familiar in order to spread the Good News. Every missionary must follow this example. We cannot seek natural comfort as a priority, but must be willing to go wherever God calls us. The Gospel must be preached to those who have not heard, regardless of the price that is to be paid.

2. The missionary must stand for truth (Acts 15:1-40). At the conclusion of this first journey, Paul came to Jerusalem for a church council. The issue at hand was whether or not newly converted Christians had to obey Jewish laws in order to be saved, as some were claiming they did. Paul, despite the fact that he himself was a Jew, insisted that salvation did not come through Jewish laws but through Christ alone. Though his stand was unpopular, he stood for what was right and the church leadership accepted his position. As a missionary, there will be times you have to stand for truth in very challenging situations. Never compromise but always be faithful to God's Word.

3. The missionary must endure persecution (Acts 16:1-19:41). Paul continued his missionary journeys and faced severe persecution. Once, in Philippi, he was beaten and placed in the inner prison, yet praised God in the midst of the situation. On many other occasions, he faced stoning, shipwreck, and a myriad of other problems. Yet he remained faithful and kept pressing forward with the message of the Gospel. As a missionary, you will suffer persecution and trials, but if you ask God for grace, He will give you a triumphant spirit and victory in the end.

4. The missionary must dearly love the people (Acts 20:1-38). Paul did not only preach to the people, he had great love for them. His heart of compassion can be seen when he raised a young man from the dead, and bid farewell to the church leaders in Ephesus. Every successful missionary must first have a deep love for the people of the land to which he is sent. This love is not just a mere sympathy but a true desire to see God change their lives and their land. Always ask God for His love to fill your heart.

So who wants to be a missionary? There is so much we can learn from Paul and his heart for God and God's people. Let's spread the ways of God throughout our world.

CHAPTER 49: PAUL (PART 3) - LEGACY (ACTS 21-TITUS)

When I was growing up, even into young adulthood before I left home to become a missionary, my mother always used to take care of all the needs of our family inside the home. She would cook dinner, wash our clothes, and make sure there was plenty of food in the house! On the rare occasions when my Mom would have to go away for a couple of days (usually to visit her mother), she would always make sure she left a lot of food behind. She would tell us what we should eat which night and make sure that we were very well taken care of - it's a great thing to have a good Mom!

The Apostle Paul left an extraordinary legacy for the Church. During his life, he invested in countless lives and left behind heavenly seed that is still bearing fruit today. He knew the importance of leaving behind a godly legacy for those who would follow him, and it is vital that we do the same. There are at least four lessons we can learn about a godly legacy from the life of Paul.

1. Paul's legacy is a display of God's longsuffering (Acts 21:1-28:31). God saved Paul from such a terrible background and used him as the leader of the Church in order to show Himself as being longsuffering (1 Timothy 1:16). God wants us to know how tremendously merciful He is. Not only did the life of Paul show longsuffering through God's patience with him, but also through the great trials Paul himself suffered. He encountered long imprisonments, shipwrecks, hunger, and even martyrdom, but he stayed faithful all of his days. Paul was a pattern of longsuffering twice over. Let's ask God to put His great longsuffering into us.

2. Paul's legacy was cemented as he wrote much of the New Testament (Romans-Philemon). The Holy Spirit used Paul to write much of the New Testament. At least thirteen (possibly fourteen) of the New Testament's twenty-seven books were written by him, and most of our proper doctrine today is framed by the thoughts in these epistles. Paul realized that his writing could take the message far further than his mouth ever could. So be faithful to write the good things that God is doing in your life and the lessons He is teaching you; it can be a great blessing to others.

3. Paul's legacy was built through changing people's lives (1 Timothy-Titus). There were countless lives changed through the Apostle Paul. He especially invested his time into two young men, Timothy and Titus. Both of them were trained by Paul to be pastors, and the instructions he gave them can be seen in the epistles that bear their names. Paul was a father in the faith to these men. We should likewise have people that we are discipling by pouring all of our lives into them. The lives we change and influence for God are the treasures we take into eternity.

4. Paul's legacy left him as one of the most influential men in the history of the world. The Apostle Paul is one of the most influential men the world has ever seen. Even secular historians rank him in the top ten of the world's most important people. Paul achieved this not because he cared about worldly honor, but rather because of the opposite; he cared only for the glory of God and thus God used him to revolutionize the world.

God is not looking for people who seek influence but for people who seek Him! And as we do this with all our heart and obey Him as the Apostle Paul did, God will use us to bring incredible change to our world. History-makers come from God-seekers.

CHAPTER 50: TIMOTHY - GOOD EXAMPLE
(ACTS 16, 1 TIMOTHY-2 TIMOTHY)

When I was fifteen years old, I got my first job at a restaurant called "Sign of the Beefcarver". Our signature item was roast beef, which was freshly sliced off a huge round of beef right in front of the customer. I started out scooping vegetables, then I became the mashed potato man, and finally I achieved the vaulted position of Beefcarver! This was about one year after I started work there, and in that year I studied the different beefcarvers to see how I should do the job. I learned that some people were good examples to mimic, and others not so good. But by copying the good examples, I became a good beefcarver myself!

Timothy was an important member of the Early Church and helper of the Apostle Paul who is an excellent example for us to follow. He served God with great passion from a young age and was still a young man when he became the bishop of the churches at Ephesus. We will consider four ways in which we should follow Timothy's good example.

1. Timothy had a good report among the believers (Acts 16:1-3). Although he was a very young man, Timothy had already developed a good reputation among all the believers in the city of Lystra. His mother and grandmother had taught him God's ways from an early age. Timothy was of such character that upon meeting him, the Apostle Paul immediately asked Timothy to come along on his missionary journey. Let us live in such a way that we have a good reputation among other believers as well. Don't seek reputation but seek God, and a good reputation will also come to you.

2. Timothy lived a life of purity, faith, and diligence (1 Timothy 1:1-6:21). Timothy was an example in all of these areas. He was known for his moral purity. Though he lived in a time of persecution, he faithfully preached God's message in the spirit of power. And he was able to teach people much older than himself the ways of God because of his study. These qualities are also vital for each of us to obtain.

3. Timothy had spiritual gifts (2 Timothy 1:1-3:17). Paul reminded Timothy to stir up the gifts that were within him. Timothy flowed in the gifts of the Spirit and had received much through the laying on of hands. He was hungry for the power of God. As young people, we should follow this example and also have a burning desire for the things of the Spirit. Let's not live on the natural plane but the supernatural, and allow God to fill us with more of His Holy Spirit.

4. Timothy faithfully served the Apostle Paul (2 Timothy 4:1-22). In his writings, Paul said that Timothy was the one man he could really trust (Philippians 2:19-23). Whenever Paul had an important job that needed to be done, he knew he could ask Timothy to go and fill the need. Even to the end of Paul's life, Timothy was the one he asked to come and minister to him. Paul was Timothy's spiritual father, and Timothy never deserted or disobeyed him. His faithfulness is an excellent example for each of us. Be faithful to those over you in the Church and serve them in humility and with consistency. When we are faithful in little things, God will promote us to great things.

Let's be like Timothy, living in such a way that we are positive examples for others. People both young and old, men and women, should be able to look at our lives for insight on how to live the Christian life. If you faithfully follow God, others will look to your example!

CHAPTER 51: PHILEMON AND ONESIMUS - RESTORED (PHILEMON 1-25)

Have you ever seen a relationship restored? I remember a famous athlete who, at one time, was very popular in my hometown of Detroit. Over time, however, he left town and became a villain in the eyes of his former fans, booed every time he played in his former hometown. After many years, however, he came back to play for Detroit and asked the fans to accept him again. The fans responded and the player once again entered into the good graces of the fans. The relationship had been restored!

One of the most famous restored relationships in the Scriptures is that between Philemon and Onesimus. This relationship is the entire theme of the Epistle of Philemon, written by the Apostle Paul. He encourages his dear friend Philemon to receive back his runaway slave, Onesimus - not as a slave, however, but as a brother. This letter reveals to us the heart of God; He is a God who loves restoring that which was lost, and there are at least four lessons we can learn about this from the lives of Philemon and Onesimus.

1. *Philemon had a good reputation, Onesimus had a bad one (Philemon 1-9).* Philemon was known throughout all the churches as being a man of good reputation. A church met inside his house and he displayed faith and love, for both God and other people. Onesimus, on the other hand, was poorly thought of. He was an unprofitable slave who had stolen from Philemon. Let us follow the example of Philemon, but also recognize in our dealings with others that a bad beginning (like Onesimus had) does not disqualify one from serving God.

2. *Philemon had been wronged by Onesimus (Philemon 10-11).* Onesimus had run away from Philemon and had stolen from him. Onesimus was now in great trouble, as runaway slaves in the Roman Empire were often crucified when they were caught, and almost always executed. As we discover later, Philemon did not take vengeance on Onesimus but forgave him. Do not take record of those who wrong you, but be quick to forgive as Philemon was.

3. *Philemon accepted Onesimus' repentance (Philemon 12-20).* Sometime after running away, Onesimus went to Rome where he met the Apostle Paul, who was imprisoned there. Paul led Onesimus to salvation and then asked Philemon to receive Onesimus back, not as a slave, but something even greater - as a brother. Philemon obeyed Paul and his relationship with Onesimus was restored. It is a beautiful story; Philemon lost Onesimus for a short season, but now they would be brothers with an eternal relationship in heaven. Be encouraged that God loves restoration! Continue to pray for the backsliders you know and always desire to see them restored.

4. *Philemon and Onesimus both had a glorious ending (Philemon 21-25).* After Philemon forgave Onesimus, church history tells us their incredible story. Philemon became Bishop of Colosse, where he served until he was martyred around 65 AD. Onesimus, the unprofitable runaway slave, became the Bishop of Ephesus - a one time thief became an important church leader! He served there until about the year 95 AD, where he was also killed by the Romans. These two men had vastly different

backgrounds, but they met the same glorious end - martyrdom for the cause of Christ. They are now celebrating their reward in heaven, and will do so for all eternity!

God loves to restore, and we should also. Don't hold grudges against others, but always look for opportunities to restore relationships. Never give up on those who have turned away from the faith, but pray for them always. God can work miracles that will blow our minds.

CHAPTER 52: APOSTLE JOHN - GOD'S LOVE (MATTHEW-JOHN, 1 JOHN-3 JOHN, REVELATION)

Have you ever gone several years without meeting someone, and then they were totally different when you saw them again? I remember one student of mine who was very small when I taught him. When we played games as a class and did activities, he was never a threatening opponent. When I saw him again after several years, however, he had become a giant, several inches taller than me! It was almost hard to recognize him as the same person.

The Apostle John is a man who was completely transformed. Today we know him as "The Apostle of Love" or "John the Beloved", but earlier in his life he certainly did not have this quality! God's love brought about tremendous change in John. God's love is His very nature, and there are four lessons about the love of God that we can learn from the life of John.

1. God's love can transform a rough character (Mark 3:17, Luke 9:51-56). Jesus called John and his brother James "sons of thunder." John was a man of action by his very nature. Once when Jesus was rejected by a certain village in Samaria, John asked Jesus if they should call down fire from heaven to consume the village and kill the people. Jesus rebuked John and told him that this desire came from the wrong spirit. John was not always a man of love, but by the end of his life he had been completely transformed. If you are not someone who is naturally inclined to love others, have hope; God can change you as completely as He changed John if you will yield your ways to His.

2. God's love brings us revelation (John 13-21). During the Last Supper, John was the disciple sitting nearest to Jesus as he had the closest relationship with the Lord. When the others wanted information, they asked John to ask Jesus for it. Jesus answered John because of the special love He had for him. Later in his life, John wrote the book of Revelation, full of visions about the future. God's love for John and John's love for God qualified him to receive visions and revelations from God. The prophetic flows from a love relationship with God.

3. God's love brings us into fellowship with Him (1 John-3 John). Towards the end of his life John wrote the three epistles of John. The constant theme in these epistles is the love of God that brings us into fellowship with Him. God wants to have a close friendship with each of His children, and John entered into that friendship with God. Ask God to increase your love for Him, and you can know God more and more.

4. God's love will bring the Church to perfection (Revelation 1-22). John wrote the book of Revelation while in prison on the island of Patmos. Revelation shows what will happen in the last days, and the climax of the book is God bringing His Church to perfection as a Bride for Himself. Revelation is a book that is commonly misunderstood; it should not be viewed as a fearful book about being left behind, but rather as an instruction on how we can be part of the glorious Church. John realized that God was going to perfect His people, and it is by the love of God that He does not leave us in our sins but leads us to holiness.

Ask God to work in your life so that you will come to true holiness and qualify to be a part of His Bride, just as He did in the life of John. Those who have been perfected will live with Christ forever and ever!

Made in the USA
Middletown, DE
16 February 2023

25033375R00064